CANADIAN CONCEPTS

Second Edition

Lynda Berish

Sandra Thibaudeau

Collège Marie-Victorin

Prentice Hall Allyn and Bacon Canada
Scarborough, Ontario

Canadian Cataloguing in Publication Data

Berish, Lynda, date
    Canadian concepts 2

2nd ed.
ISBN 0-13-591694-1

1. English language—Textbooks for second language learners.*
2. English Language—Grammar.   3. English language—Grammar—
Problems, exercises, etc.   I. Thibaudeau, Sandra, date.   II. Title.

PE1128.B47 1996   428.2'4   C96-931531-7

Allyn and Bacon, Inc., Needham Heights, Massachusetts
Prentice-Hall, Inc., Upper Saddle River, New Jersey
Prentice-Hall International (UK) Limited, London
Prentice-Hall of Australia, Pty., Ltd., Sydney
Prentice-Hall Hispanoamericana, S. A., Mexico
Prentice-Hall of India Private Limited, New Delhi
Prentice-Hall of Japan, Inc., Tokyo
Prentice-Hall of Southeast Asia (PTE) Ltd., Singapore
Simon & Schuster Asia Private Limited, Singapore
Editora Prentice-Hall do Brasil Ltda., Rio de Janeiro

ISBN 0-13-591694-1

Acquisitions editor: Dominique Roberge
Developmental editor: Marta Tomins
Production editor: Elynor Kagan
Editorial assistant: Rita Self
Production coordinator: Sharon Houston
Design: Monica Kompter
Layout: Joseph Chin
Text illustrations: Paul McCusker
Unit opening illlustrations: Carole Giguère
Cover image: A.G.E./First Light, "Rue St. Louis, Quebec City"

Printed and bound in Canada

1 2 3 4 5   99 98 97 96

Visit the Prentice Hall Canada web site! Send us
your comments, browse our catalogues, and more.
www.phcanada.com Or reach us through e-mail
at **phabinfo_pubcanada@prenhall.com**

To the many teachers we've met across Canada,
for their valuable input, and to their students.

CONTENTS

<table>
<tr><td>LISTENING ACTIVITIES</td><td>GAMES AND ACTIVITIES</td></tr>
<tr><td>1. I'm Pleased To Meet You</td><td>Picture Crossword
Word Search
Game: Mystery Person</td></tr>
<tr><td>2. Names and Places
3. How Are You Today?</td><td>Game: Numbers Tic-Tac-Toe
Quick Review</td></tr>
<tr><td>4. What's the Weather Like Today?
5. Where Were You Yesterday?</td><td>Categories
Find Someone</td></tr>
<tr><td>6. What a Nice Family
7. Are These Your Friends?</td><td>Opposites
Crossword Puzzle: Family Members</td></tr>
</table>

<table>
<tr><td>

18. What Do You Do?
19. Applying For a Job

</td><td>

Puzzle: Jobs
Game: Jobs Tic-Tac-Toe

</td></tr>
</table>

The World

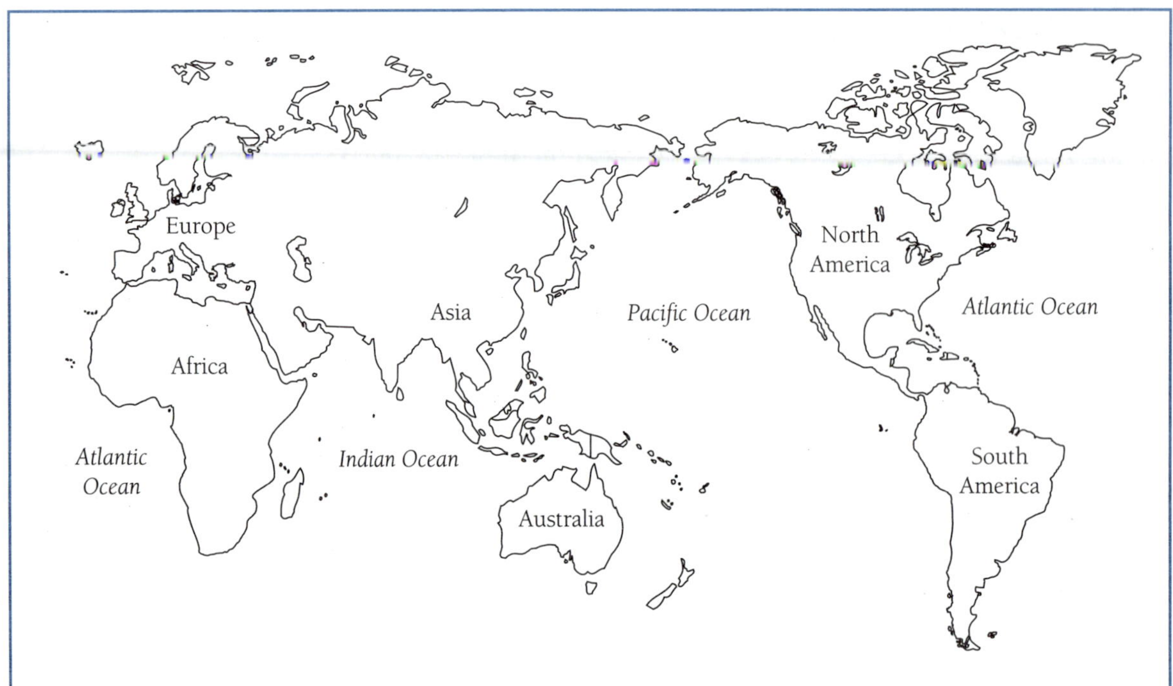

Canada

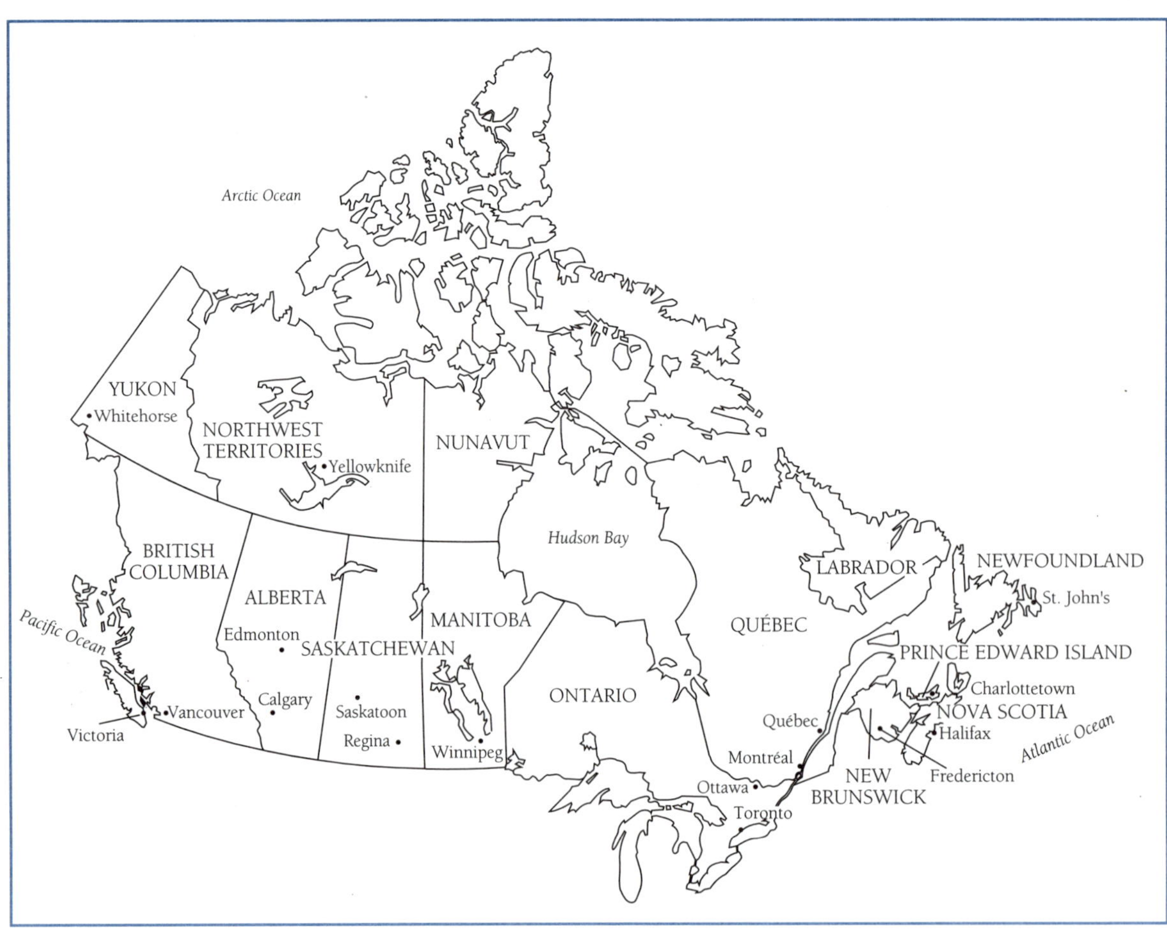

TO THE TEACHER

The *Canadian Concepts* Series

The new edition of the popular *Canadian Concepts* series retains the Canadian focus designed to help students feel at home and integrate into the community. In the new edition, exercises and activities have been graded and, in some cases, refocussed to provide a careful build-up of skills throughout the series. *Canadian Concepts 1* is paced to accommodate the needs of post-literacy students, while *Canadian Concepts 2* moves ahead to introduce new vocabulary and grammatical structures at a faster pace. *Canadian Concepts 3* provides a richer field of vocabulary and a greater degree of challenge while reinforcing the themes of the lower levels. *Canadian Concepts 4, 5,* and *6* integrate video materials on Canadian themes.

The *Canadian Concepts* series uses a communicative approach. The method offers productive strategies for language learning based on student-centred interaction. Many new activities, games, and opportunities for speaking have been incorporated into the series to encourage maximum student participation in classroom activities. The pedagogical model presents students with challenging listening or reading input, leading them through pre-activities and strategies that make the input comprehensible. In addition to these fluency-building activities, dictation, grammar, spelling, and vocabulary work focus on improving students' accuracy.

Canadian Concepts 2

Canadian Concepts 2 reviews and expands on themes from *Canadian Concepts 1*. It is intended for students at the false-beginner stage, and provides ample practice with basic functional language in all skill areas, together with appropriate grammar. Students focus on survival English topics in meaningful contexts. The cast of characters from *Canadian Concepts 1* continues in this book, to provide continuity.

Students gain confidence to function in English from the survival topics and cultural information presented in the book. They are motivated to use their new skills in the real world through the Community Contact Tasks. Throughout the book, language is carefully graded to help students become more proficient and more confident as they move through the text.

Canadian Concepts 2 is made up of ten self-contained thematic units. Core activities focus on simple dialogues and reading texts. They are designed to provide students with the language they need for their daily lives. Follow-up activities recycle language and concepts and lead the students into meaningful practice contexts.

Listening, speaking, reading, writing, grammar, pronunciation, and vocabulary-development exercises are integrated into all units. Clear illustrations lend valuable visual support. Each unit concludes with Ten-Minute Games and Activities that review and extend new vocabulary and structures.

Teachers and students will appreciate the lively appearance and simple format of the materials. They will also enjoy browsing through Canadian Capsules that provide background information on Canada. The audio cassette tape has been recorded with concern for natural Canadian speech patterns. Worksheets to accompany many of the activities in *Canadian Concepts 2* are provided in the Teacher's Manual, with permission to photocopy.

KEY TO SYMBOLS

 Listening activity

 Reading activity

 Writing activity

 Work with a partner

 Work in a group

 Journal activity

Teacher's Manual

A comprehensive Teacher's Manual provides step-by-step instructions keyed to the student book, answer keys, tape scripts, and teaching notes. Teaching tips and suggestions for optional activities for use in multi-level classrooms are incorporated.

Detailed teacher's notes are included to clarify the intention of activities and to make suggestions for promoting interaction in the classroom. These ideas will be appreciated by new teachers, while experienced teachers will find that the materials lend themselves to flexible interpretation and accommodate individual teaching styles.

At the End of the Course

Students who successfully complete this level will be ready for *Canadian Concepts 3*, which builds on basic themes with a wide variety of activities and discussion topics.

NICE TO MEET YOU

THE ALPHABET

A B C D E F G H I J K L M N O P Q R S T U V W X Y Z

a b c d e f g h i j k l m n o p q r s t u v w x y x

𝒜 ℬ 𝒞 𝒟 ℰ ℱ 𝒢 ℋ ℐ 𝒥 𝒦 ℒ ℳ 𝒩 𝒪 𝒫 𝒬 ℛ 𝒮 𝒯 𝒰 𝒱 𝒲 𝒳 𝒴 𝒵

a b c d e f g h i j k l m n o p q r s t u v w x y z

A Practise with the teacher. Say the letters of the alphabet.

B Circle the letters that the teacher says. Use the worksheet.

1. a) a
   b) e

2. a) g
   b) j

3. a) i
   b) e

4. a) k
   b) q

5. a) v
   b) w

6. a) l
   b) r

7. a) b
   b) p

8. a) x
   b) y

9. a) z
   b) s

10. a) f
    b) s

NICE TO MEET YOU

A   Practise with the teacher.

B   Practise with a partner.

GREETINGS

Mr. (mister)	for a man
Mrs. (missus)	for a married woman
Miss	for an unmarried woman
Ms. (miz)	for a woman in business
Dr. (doctor)	for a doctor

Say: Hello, Mr. Banon.
Hi, Michel.

Say: Hello, Ms. Martin.
Hi, Kate.

Right: Hi, Michel.
Hello, Mr. Banon.

Right: Hi, Kate.
Hello, Ms. Martin.

Right: Hi, Olga.
Hello, Mrs. Kuslov.

Say: Hello, Mrs. Kuslov.
Hi, Olga.

Wrong: Hello Mr. Michel.
Hello Ms. Olga.

Wrong: Hello teacher.
Hello Ms. teacher.
Hello Mr. teacher.
Hello my teacher.

A Look at the pictures on page 2. Write a greeting for each person.

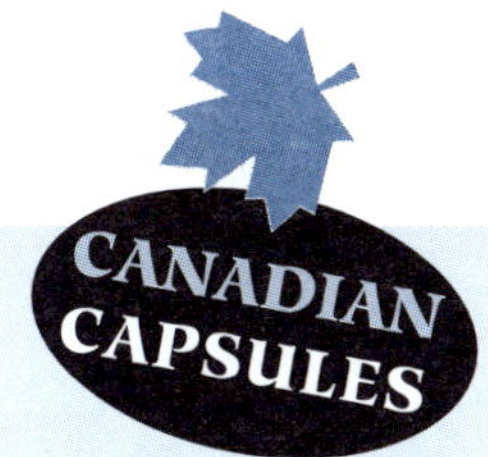

CANADIAN CAPSULES

In Canada, most people have two or three names. They have a first name and a last name (or family name). Sometimes they also have a middle name.

I'M PLEASED TO MEET YOU

LISTENING ACTIVITY 1

A Practise with the teacher.

B Practise with a partner.

 **C** Listen and complete the conversations. Use the worksheet.

Michel and Carlos

Michel: Hello. I'm Michel.

Carlos: Hi Michel. I'm Carlos. Nice to ___________ you.

Michel: It's nice to meet ___________ too, Carlos.

Lili and Mona

Lili: Hi. I'm Lili.

Mona: Hello, Lili. _________ to meet you. I'm Mona.

Lili: Hello Mona. I'm ___________ to meet you too.

Jun and Olga

Jun: Hello. I'm Jun.

Olga: Hi Jun. I'm ___________ to meet you. I'm Olga.

Jun: I'm ___________ to meet you too, Olga.

 **D** Practise the conversations with a partner.

WHERE ARE YOU FROM?

A   Practise with the teacher.

B   Practise with a partner.

C   Read the sentences with a partner.

    Kate: Hello. I'm Kate Martin. I'm from Canada.

    Mona: Hello. My name is Mona. I'm from Egypt.

  Michel: Hi. I'm Michel. I'm from Haiti.

     Ana: Hello. I'm Ana, and this is Carlos. We're from Mexico.

    Max: Hi. My name is Max, and this is Olga. We're from Russia.

    Jun: Hi. I'm Jun. I'm from Korea.

    Lili: Hello. My name is Lili. I'm from China.

D   Work with a partner. Answer "yes" or "no."

1.   Max is from Haiti.

2.   Jun is from Korea.

3.   Lili is from Japan.

4.   Ana and Carlos are from Mexico.

5.   Mona is from Haiti.

6.   Olga and Max are from Russia.

7.   Michel is from Egypt.

SPELL THE COUNTRIES

Do you know these countries?

Work with a partner. Complete the names of the countries. Use your notebook. Then listen to the teacher to check the letters.

1.   T __ r k __ y

2.   A __ g e __ t __ __ a

3.   J __ p __ n

4.   P __ l a __ d

5.   C __ n __ d __

6.   F __ a __ c e

7.   B __ a z i __

8.   I __ a __ y

9.   V __ e __ n __ m

10. P __ r __

11. M __ l __ y s __ __

12. __ r __ e c e

13. E __ S __ l v __ d __ r

14. I __ d o __ e s __ a

MEET THE STUDENTS IN YOUR CLASS

Practise with the teacher.

Say:

Hi, I'm _______________.

Hello, my name is _______________.

Where are you from?

Answer:

Nice to meet you.

I'm pleased to meet you.

I'm from _______________.

TALK ABOUT IT

Walk around the class. Meet the students. Have the conversation with six
students.

SURVEY: PEOPLE IN THE CLASS

Make a chart. Talk to six new people. Write the information in the chart.

First name	Last name	Country

CANADIAN CAPSULES

Sometimes people in Canada give their children the same first name as
another person in the family—for example, a grandparent or an aunt or
uncle. Sometimes they just choose names they like for their children.

GRAMMAR FOCUS   Subject Pronouns

A   Write the pronoun.

> Kate Martin   **she**

1. Michel Banon
2. Olga and Max
3. Mona
4. a book
5. Mr. Lopez

6. the teacher
7. Lili Han
8. a man
9. a woman
10. students

B   Which pronouns are wrong? Correct them.

1. Lili is a woman. **It** is from China.
2. Olga and Max are from Russia. **We** are students.
3. Kate is a teacher. **She** is from Canada.
4. Michel is a man. **She** is from Haiti.
5. This is my book. **He** is big.
6. Jun is a man. **He** is from Korea.
7. Ana and Carlos are from Mexico. **He** are happy.
8. Mona and Lili are women. **She** are friends.

 **GRAMMAR FOCUS**   **Verb "Be"**

Verb *Be*
I am
you are
he is
she is
it is
we are
you are
they are

Use the verb **be** with:

Names	Ages	Jobs
I am Ana.	He is 18 years old.	I am a student.
He is Michel.	She is 25.	They are teachers.
Nationality	**Location**	**Description**
I am Canadian.	They are from Mexico.	He is old.
He is Japanese.	It is in the classroom.	She is tall.
Emotions		
We are happy.		
They are tired.		

 Use **be** for age. Use **be** for names.

GRAMMAR FOCUS   **Verb "Be": Contractions**

Contractions are short forms for speaking and for informal writing.

Full form	Contraction
I am	I'm
you are	you're
he is	he's
she is	she's
it is	it's
we are	we're
you are	you're
they are	they're

Hi, I'm from China.
This is my friend. He's from France.

A Write the pronoun and the verb. Use contractions.

> (Max) __________ from Russia.   **He's** from Russia.

1.   (The students) __________ from Mexico.

2.   (The school) __________ new.

3.   (The girls) __________ friends.

4.   (Toronto) __________ in Canada.

5.   (I) __________ a student.

6.   (Michel) __________ from Haiti.

7.   (The room) __________ small.

8.   (Mona) __________ tall.

9.   (Lili and I) __________ students.

10.   (The book) __________ big.

B Some sentences are wrong. Correct verbs that are wrong.

1.   The friends be happy.

2.   He are 19 years old.

3.   The school is old.

4.   I be from Russia.

5.   You is 26 years old.

6.   We are friends.

7.   The woman is tall.

8.   The classroom be big.

9.   They are teachers.

10.   We be students.

IN THE CLASSROOM

 Look at the picture. Give the answers.

1. Write three words with six letters.

2. Write five words with five letters.

3. Write two words that begin with the letter **P**.

4. Write three words with three letters.

5. Write three words that begin with the letter **C**.

6. Write three words with four letters.

7. Write two words that begin with the letter **W**.

8. Write two words that begin with the letter **B**.

THINGS IN THE CLASSROOM

Look at the pictures. Practise with the teacher. Say the words.

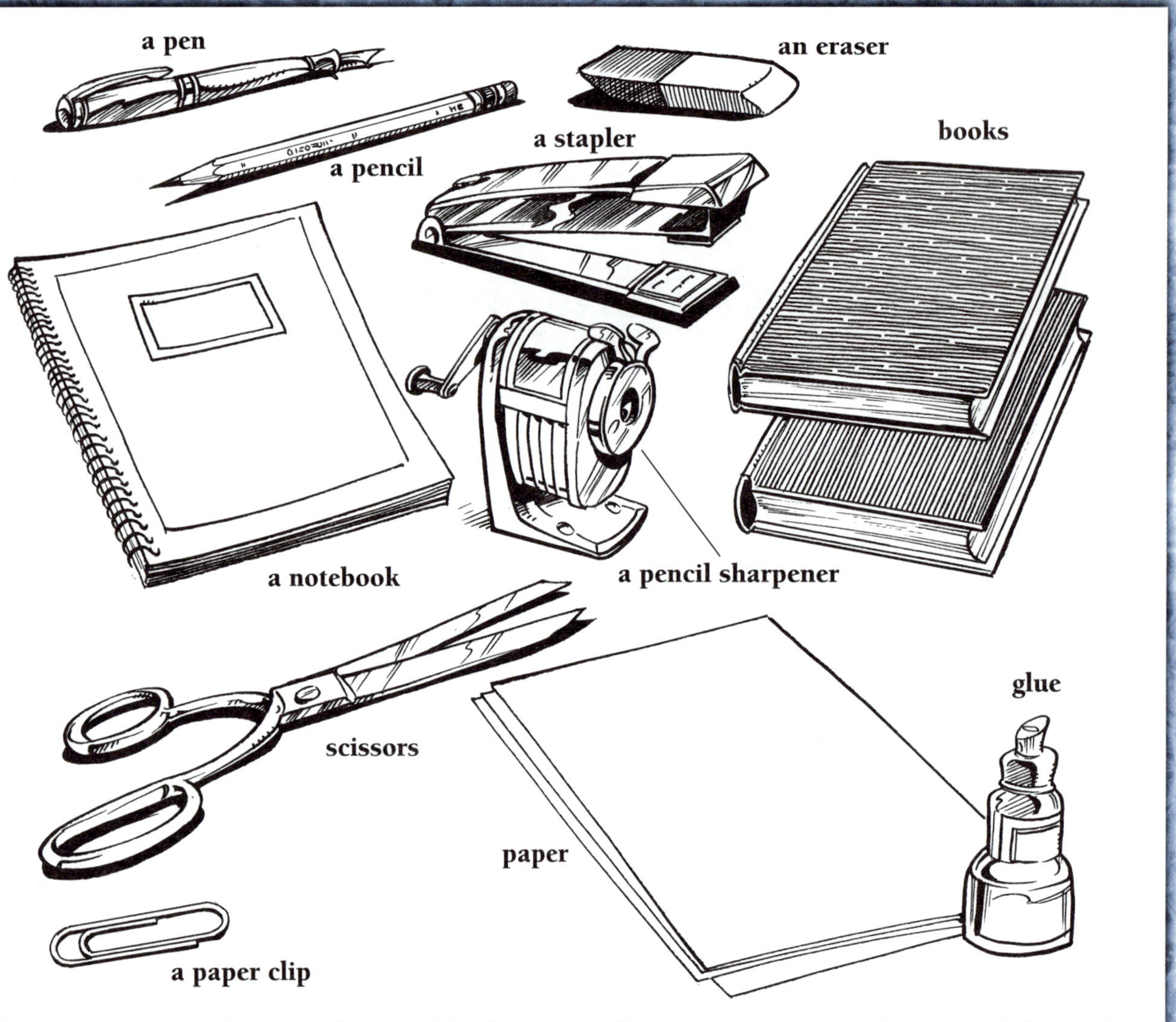

TALK ABOUT IT

Do you have these things? Work in a group. Show your group the things you have.

Ask: Do you have…

Answer: I have…   I don't have…

 **Plurals**

Use **s** after a noun for the plural form.

1 student   3 student**s**

person   people

man   men

woman   women

child   children

A Write the plurals.

1.	teacher	7.	name
2.	student	8.	pencil
3.	child	9.	woman
4.	person	10.	man
5.	book	11.	classroom
6.	room	12.	girl

B Some plurals are wrong. Correct them.

1. Lili and Kate are woman.

2. The childrens are in the classroom.

3. There are two schools on the street.

4. Jun and Michel are friends.

5. We are student from Mexico.

6. Matthew and Tom are childs.

7. They are old book.

8. The two women are happy.

9. Fifteen peoples are in the class.

10. The room are small.

JOURNAL

A Read the sentences. Close your book. Listen to the teacher. Write the sentences in your notebook.

I am Lili Han. I am a woman. I am from China.

B Buy a notebook. This is your journal. Write sentences about yourself.

TEN-MINUTE GAMES AND ACTIVITIES

Picture Crossword

Write the words in the puzzle. Use the worksheet.

Across

3

4

5

7

8

10

Down

1

2

3

6

9

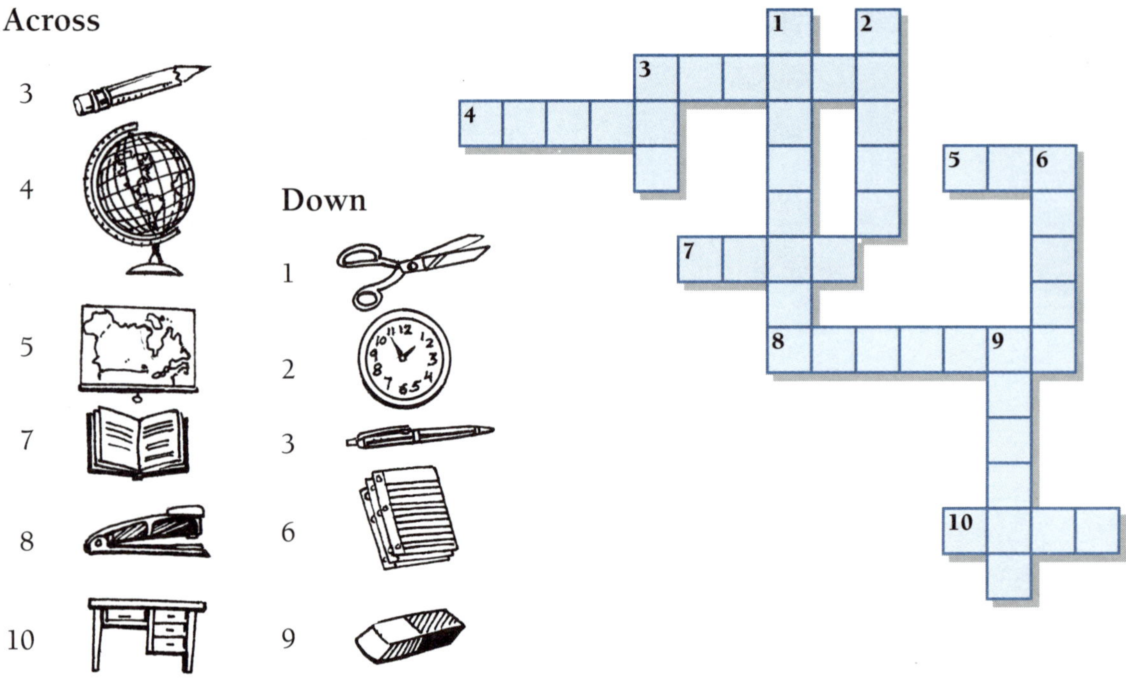

Word Search

Find these words in the puzzle. Circle the words. Use the worksheet.

pen pencil eraser notebook clock globe stapler scissors
map glue book sharpener

```
e  i  g  h  g  o  b  m  a  p  e  y  c
p  e  n  c  i  l  b  e  y  c  q  b  a
b  v  z  e  b  o  o  k  e  q  t  w  t
i  q  t  s  t  a  p  l  e  r  e  c  v
e  y  c  y  s  c  i  s  s  o  r  s  z
g  l  o  b  e  i  q  b  c  w  t  x  t
w  v  w  b  s  h  a  r  p  e  n  e  r
e  y  c  o  b  g  l  u  e  q  b  x  t
e  b  s  c  l  o  c  k  a  o  p  n  n
m  w  t  n  o  t  e  b  o  o  k  z  e
t  s  i  x  t  e  r  a  s  e  r  o  x
o  e  b  x  e (p  e  n) b  s  e  b  z
```

Game: Mystery Person

The teacher writes the following information on the board:

> I am a… (man/woman)
>
> I am from…
>
> My language is…

Students copy and complete the information about themselves on a card or piece of paper.

Students then put their cards in a box. The teacher chooses a card and reads it. The students guess the name of the person who wrote the card.

2

PEOPLE AND PLACES

SAYING NUMBERS

 **A** Practise with the teacher.

1	one	26	twenty-six	51	fifty-one	76	seventy-six
2	two	27	twenty-seven	52	fifty-two	77	seventy-seven
3	three	28	twenty-eight	53	fifty-three	78	seventy-eight
4	four	29	twenty-nine	54	fifty-four	79	seventy-nine
5	five	30	thirty	55	fifty-five	80	eighty
6	six	31	thirty-one	56	fifty-six	81	eighty-one
7	seven	32	thirty-two	57	fifty-seven	82	eighty-two
8	eight	33	thirty-three	58	fifty-eight	83	eighty-three
9	nine	34	thirty-four	59	fifty-nine	84	eighty-four
10	ten	35	thirty-five	60	sixty	85	eighty-five
11	eleven	36	thirty-six	61	sixty-one	86	eighty-six
12	twelve	37	thirty-seven	62	sixty-two	87	eighty-seven
13	thirteen	38	thirty-eight	63	sixty-three	88	eighty-eight
14	fourteen	39	thirty-nine	64	sixty-four	89	eighty-nine
15	fifteen	40	forty	65	sixty-five	90	ninety
16	sixteen	41	forty-one	66	sixty-six	91	ninety-one
17	seventeen	42	forty-two	67	sixty-seven	92	ninety-two
18	eighteen	43	forty-three	68	sixty-eight	93	ninety-three
19	nineteen	44	forty-four	69	sixty-nine	94	ninety-four
20	twenty	45	forty-five	70	seventy	95	ninety-five
21	twenty-one	46	forty-six	71	seventy-one	96	ninety-six
22	twenty-two	47	forty-seven	72	seventy-two	97	ninety-seven
23	twenty-three	48	forty-eight	73	seventy-three	98	ninety-eight
24	twenty-four	49	forty-nine	74	seventy-four	99	ninety-nine
25	twenty-five	50	fifty	75	seventy-five	100	one hundred

B Listen to the teacher. Circle the numbers you hear. Use the worksheet.

1. a) 14	11. a) 68
b) 40	b) 88
2. a) 6	12. a) 91
b) 66	b) 90
3. a) 76	13. a) 21
b) 67	b) 29
4. a) 12	14. a) 16
b) 11	b) 15
5. a) 90	15. a) 9
b) 19	b) 29
6. a) 50	16. a) 7
b) 15	b) 27
7. a) 79	17. a) 80
b) 71	b) 18
8. a) 28	18. a) 5
b) 86	b) 25
9. a) 37	19. a) 40
b) 73	b) 30
10. a) 85	20. a) 96
b) 25	b) 26

C Write the numbers the teacher says. Use your notebook.

TELEPHONE NUMBERS

A Practise with the teacher.

B   Circle the number you hear. Use the worksheet.

1. a) 857-5498
    b) 857-5998

2. a) 890-3141
    b) 890-3114

3. a) 936-4167
    b) 936-4176

4. a) 212-4510
    b) 212-5401

5. a) 634-8965
    b) 634-9856

6. a) 321-5111
    b) 312-5111

7. a) 798-4590
    b) 987-4509

8. a) 731-5621
    b) 731-2156

9. a) 856-0902
    b) 865-9020

10. a) 426-1335
    b) 426-3115

C   Practise with a partner. Say the phone numbers.

836-8965	812-1277	738-1298
428-9019	326-1367	429-1287
273-9864	870-4252	738-0223

ADDRESSES

A   Practise with the teacher.

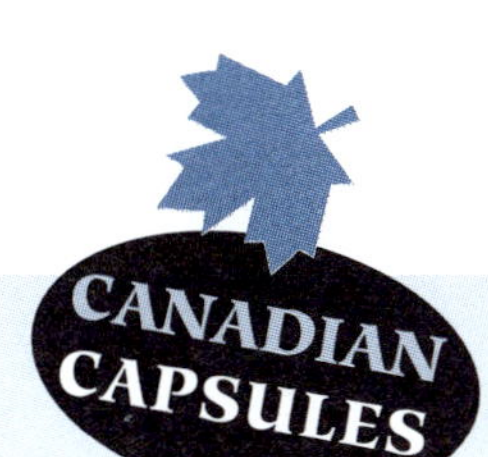

CANADIAN CAPSULES

Canadians talk on the telephone a lot. Perhaps it is because some people don't like to go outside when it is cold!

B   Practise the addresses with a partner.

438 Coolbrook	3421 Pine
789 Maple	7890 Eglinton
3840 Dufferin	2132 Granville
873 Steeles	2156 Oakview
3678 Clark	5120 Robson

NAMES AND PLACES

LISTENING ACTIVITY 2

A   Match the question with the answer.

1.	What is your name?	a)	It is 387-9980.
2.	Where are you from?	b)	It is Carlos Lopez.
3.	What is your telephone number?	c)	I'm from Mexico.
4.	What is your address?	d)	3884 Bay

B   Listen and complete the chart. Use the worksheet.

First name	Last name	Address	Phone number
Lili		4389 Clark	879-4589
	Lopez	Bay	349-0976
Michel		324	
Kate	Martin	Tudor	
	Aziz	3789	
Jun	Kim	Linton	
Olga	Kuslov	6792	980-5647

C   Practise with the teacher.

What's your first name?	Julie
Can you spell it please?	J-u-l-i-e
What's your last name?	Kent
Can you spell it please?	K-e-n-t
What's your address?	4289 Appleton
Can you spell it please?	A-p-p-l-e-t-o-n
What's your phone number?	721-0931
Can you repeat it please?	721-0931

SURVEY: PERSONAL INFORMATION

Copy the chart in your notebook. Introduce yourself to six new people in the class. Complete the chart.

First name	Last name	Address	Phone number

"Be": Question Form

For questions with **be**, put the verb before the subject.

> They **are** students.   **Are** they students?

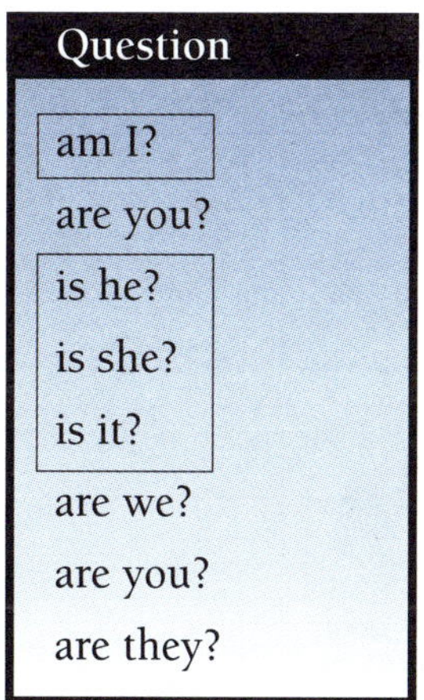

 Write a question.

> She is Canadian.   **Is she Canadian?**

1. They are Taiwanese.
2. Mr. Lopez is Mexican.
3. She is a teacher.
4. We are students.
5. Lili is Chinese.

6. Kate is Canadian.
7. She is a doctor.
8. I am late.
9. Max is tall.
10. They are happy.

B   Write ten questions about the information in the boxes.

> Is Jun Korean?
>
> Is Michel a cook?

Family Name:	Banon
First name:	Michel
Nationality:	Haitian
Occupation (job):	cook

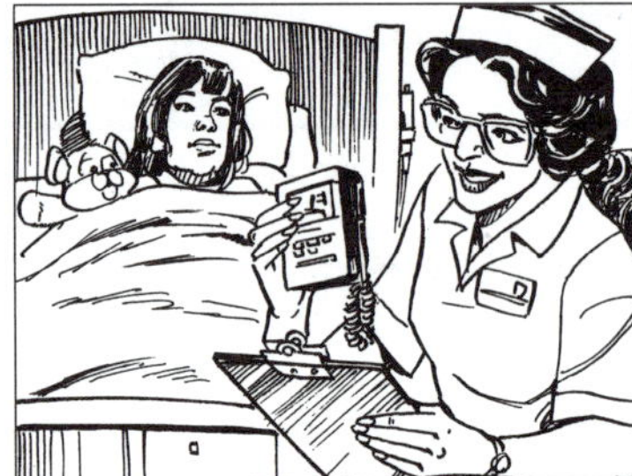

Family name:	Aziz
First name:	Mona
Nationality:	Egyptian
Occupation (job):	nurse

Family Name:	Kuslov
First Name:	Max
Nationality:	Russian
Occupation (job):	taxi driver

Family Name:	Han
First Name:	Lili
Nationality:	Chinese
Occupation (job):	bank teller

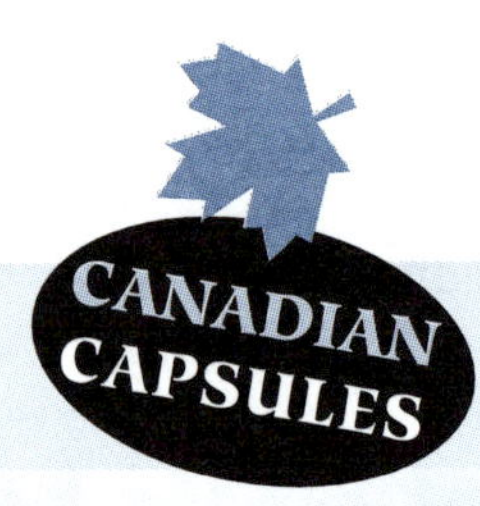
CANADIAN CAPSULES

In many towns and cities in Canada, there is one number to call in an emergency: 911. Check the emergency number in your city or town.

NATIONALITIES

Match the country and the nationality.

> Canada   Canadian

1.	Spain	a)	Moroccan
2.	Greece	b)	Vietnamese
3.	England	c)	Peruvian
4.	China	d)	Russian
5.	Korea	e)	American
6.	Morocco	f)	Spanish
7.	Peru	g)	English
8.	United States	h)	Chinese
9.	Vietnam	i)	Greek
10.	Russia	j)	Korean

"Be": Negative

For negative statements with **be**, add **not** after the verb.

> They **are not** students.

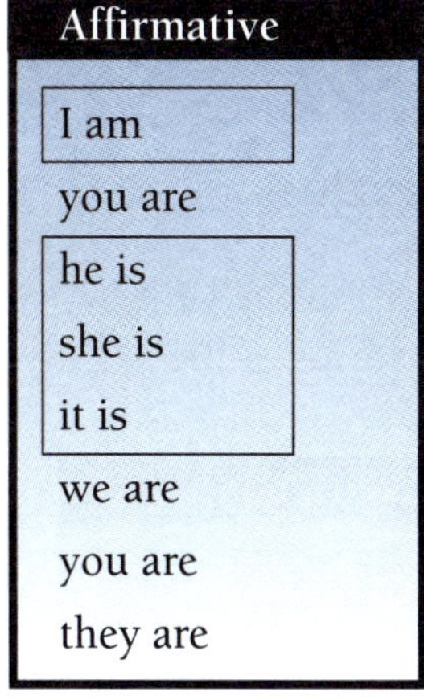

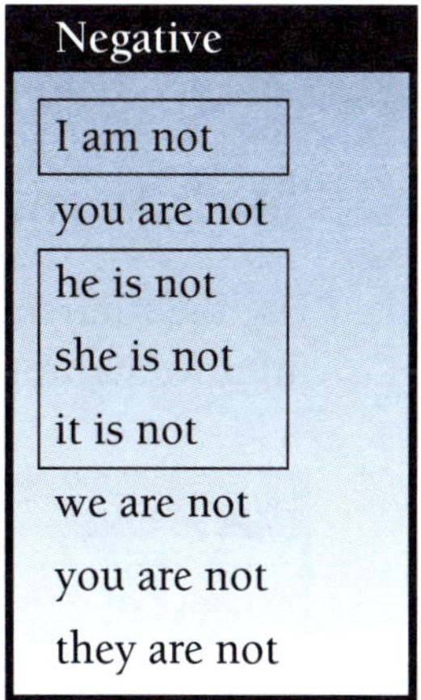

A Write the negative.

> We are English.   **We are not English.**

1. I am Canadian.
2. He is American.
3. They are Japanese.
4. She is French.
5. We are Korean.
6. She is Australian.
7. He is Italian.
8. They are Turkish.
9. She is Chinese.
10. They are Brazilian.

B Complete the sentences.

> I am **not** English.

1. Ms. Aziz is __________ Moroccan.
2. __________ am not American.
3. Lili __________ not Japanese.
4. Ms. Martin is __________ Australian.
5. We __________ not Italian.
6. They are __________ Chinese.
7. I __________ not French.
8. He is __________ Canadian.
9. They __________ not Lebanese.
10. She __________ not Greek.

GRAMMAR FOCUS

"Be": Negative Contraction

Use the contraction (short form) of the verb **be** + **not** for speaking or informal writing. Look at two forms of the negative contraction.

Full form	Contraction A	Contraction B
I am not	I'm not	Ø
you are not	you're not	you aren't
he is not	he's not	he isn't
she is not	she's not	she isn't
it is not	it's not	it isn't
we are not	we're not	we aren't
you are not	you're not	you aren't
they are not	they're not	they aren't

A Write the contraction. Use Contraction Form A.

> we are not   **we're not**

1. I am not
2. he is not
3. you are not
4. it is not
5. they are not
6. she is not

B Correct the information. Use a subject pronoun and the word in brackets. Follow the example.

> Kate is American. (Canada) **She isn't American. She's Canadian.**

1. Lili is Japanese. (Chinese)
2. The classroom is small. (big)
3. The students are French. (American)
4. I'm in England. (Canada)
5. My friends and I are teachers. (students)
6. Max is a cook. (a taxi driver)
7. Mona is a bank teller. (a nurse)
8. Pedro is a girl. (a boy)
9. You are Canadian. (American)
10. The cat is big. (small)

GRAMMAR FOCUS

"Be": Short Answers

It is not necessary to answer with a sentence when you speak. Use **yes** or **no** + subject and verb to answer questions.

Question: Is he happy?

Short Answer: Yes, he is. (happy)

A   Look at the pictures. Choose the answers.

1.   She's sad.   Yes, she is.   No, she isn't.

2.   He is a cook.   Yes, he is.   No, he isn't.

3.   They're students.   Yes, they are.   No, they aren't.

4.   I'm in France.   Yes, you are.   No, you aren't.

5.   We're hot.   Yes, you are.   No, you aren't.

6.   They are happy.   Yes, they are.   No, they aren't.

7.   He is a taxi driver.   Yes, he is.   No, he isn't.

8.   You are bank tellers.   Yes, we are.   No, we aren't.

9.   She is a child.   Yes, she is.   No, she isn't.

10.   You're a nurse.   Yes, I am.   No, I'm not.

HOW ARE YOU TODAY?

LISTENING ACTIVITY 3

A   Practise with the teacher.

B   Practise with a partner.

Mona: Hi, Lili. How are you today?

Lili: Fine thanks. And you?

Mona: I'm fine.

Lili: Well, have a nice day.

Mona: You too.

C   Listen and write the words. Use the worksheet.

Michel and Carlos

Michel: Hi, Carlos. How are __________ today?

Carlos: I'm OK. How are you?

Michel: I'm __________.

Carlos: Well, have __________ nice day.

Michel: Thanks. You __________!

Kate and Mona

Kate: Hello, Mona. How __________ you today?

Mona: I'm __________, Kate. How are __________?

Kate: I'm OK.

Mona: Well, have a __________ day.

Kate: You __________!

Olga and Jun

Olga: Hi, Jun. How __________ you today?

Jun: Fine __________. How are __________?

Olga: I'm fine.

Jun: Well, have __________ nice day.

Olga: You too.

D   Practise the conversations with a partner.

Walk around the classroom. Talk to six people. Practise the conversation. Don't use your book.

JOURNAL

 **A**   Read the sentences. Close your book. Listen to the teacher. Write the sentences in your notebook.

> I'm Michel. I'm from Haiti. I'm a cook. My phone number is 879-4589. My address is 4389 Clark Street.

  **B**   Write five sentences about yourself.

TEN-MINUTE GAMES AND ACTIVITIES

Game: Numbers Tic-Tac-Toe

The class works in two teams: Team **X** and Team **O**.

A student from Team **X** begins by choosing a square on the grid below and reading the contents aloud. If he or she reads correctly, the teacher marks an **X** on the matching square on a tic-tac-toe grid on the board.

A student from Team **O** selects a square and reads it aloud in the same way. If he or she reads correctly, the teacher marks an **O** in the matching square.

The first team to get three **X**s or three **O**s in a row wins. The rows can be vertical, horizontal, or diagonal.

1.

620 Maple Street	V1L 2X5	19
37	640 Tudor	861-2212
873-4001	M2Y 3C7	919

2.

4590 Granville	731-9088	55
P3C G2T	389-5671	4180 Oak
515	H4R lY8	K1Y 3H7

Quick Review

Work with a partner. The first pair to have a full set of correct answers
wins.

Find:

1. A country that begins with the letter **G**

2. Three countries that begin with the letter **A**

3. A country and a language that begin with the letter **S**

4. A country that has five letters in its name

5. A large city in Canada that begins with the letter **T**

6. A language that begins with the letter **E**

7. A large city in Canada that has nine letters

8. A number that has four letters in it

9. A country that is in South America

10. Two numbers that begin with the letter **F**

DAYS AND DATES

DAYS OF THE WEEK

A Work with a partner. Complete the days of the week.

M __ n d __ y
T __ e s __ a y
W __ __ n e __ d a __
T __ u __ s __ a y
F __ i d __ __ __
S a __ __ u r d __ y
S __ n __ a y

January						
Sunday	Monday	Tuesday	Wednesday	Thursday	Friday	Saturday
	1	2	3	4	5	6
7	8	9	10	11	12	13
14	15	16	17	18	19	20
21	22	23	24	25	26	27
28	29	30	31			

B Read the sentences. Write the names of the days that:

1. have six letters
2. begin with the letter **t**
3. begin with the letter **s**
4. have eight letters
5. have nine letters
6. have seven letters
7. are the weekend

MONTHS OF THE YEAR

A   Write the letters that your teacher says.

B   Work with a partner. Say the months.

C   Put the months of the year in order. Start with January.

ORDINAL NUMBERS

A   Say the numbers with the teacher.

1st first	11th eleventh	21st twenty-first
2nd second	12th twelfth	22nd twenty-second
3rd third	13th thirteenth	23rd twenty-third
4th fourth	14th fourteenth	24th twenty-fourth
5th fifth	15th fifteenth	25th twenty-fifth
6th sixth	16th sixteenth	26th twenty-sixth
7th seventh	17th seventeenth	27th twenty-seventh
8th eighth	18th eighteenth	28th twenty-eighth
9th ninth	19th nineteenth	29th twenty-ninth
10th tenth	20th twentieth	30th thirtieth
		31st thirty-first

B   Listen and circle the answers. Use the worksheet.

1. a) twelfth
    b) twentieth

2. a) ninth
    b) nineteenth

3. a) first
    b) thirty-first

4. a) tenth
    b) seventeenth

5. a) fifteenth
    b) twenty-fifth

6. a) forty-seventh
    b) seventh

7. a) twenty-second
    b) second

8. a) sixteenth
    b) fourteenth

9. a) eleventh
    b) eighth

10. a) eighteenth
     b) eighth

C   Listen and circle the answers. Use the worksheet.

1.	a) 28th	6.	a) 1st
	b) 8th		b) 11th
2.	a) 19th	7.	a) 21st
	b) 29th		b) 1st
3.	a) 5th	8.	a) 2nd
	b) 65th		b) 22nd
4.	a) 14th	9.	a) 4th
	b) 24th		b) 14th
5.	a) 30th	10.	a) 25th
	b) 13th		b) 35th

D   Complete the sentences with ordinal numbers.

> March is the **third** month of the year.

1. Monday is the ________________ day of the week.

2. April is the ________________ month of the year.

3. October is the ________________ month of the year.

4. The fourth day of the week is ________________.

5. The twelfth month of the year is ________________.

6. The ________________ month of the year is November.

7. The second month of the year is ________________.

8. May is the ________________ month of the year.

9. The third day of the week is ________________.

10. The ________________ month of the year is February.

11. The tenth month of the year is ________________.

12. August is the ________________ month of the year.

CANADIAN CAPSULES

Most Canadians think of summer as the time between two long weekends: July 1, which is Canada Day, and Labour Day in early September. In many parts of Canada, however, summer weather can start in May and continue until mid-September.

BIRTHDAYS

A   Write the date (month and day) of your birthday.

> My birthday is July 21st.

B   Work in pairs to exchange information.

> **Partner A:** Use the information below.
>
> **Partner B:** Turn to page 48.

Partner A

1. Work with another "Partner A." Write the ages for the people on the left side of the chart.

2. Then work with a "Partner B" to find the ages of the people on the right. Give your partner information about the people on the left.

   Ask: How old is Mark?

   Say: Tara is _______ years old.

	Date of birth			Age		Age
	Day	Month	Year			
Tara	10	05	1979	______	Mark	______
John	7	06	1949	______	Milly	______
Ralph	11	07	1915	______	Scott	______
Rick	15	03	1960	______	Melanie	______
Julia	8	08	1993	______	Lisa	______
Andrea	1	03	1983	______	Kelly	______
Miriam	16	05	1925	______	Bruce	______

SURVEY: BIRTHDAYS

Interview eight people in the class. Write their birthdays in the chart.

Ask: When is your birthday?

Answer: It is _______________ .

Name	Birthday
1.	
2.	
3.	
4.	
5.	
6.	
7.	
8.	

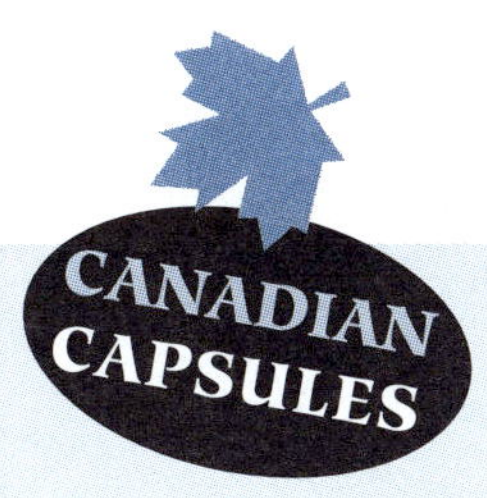

CANADIAN CAPSULES

It is a custom for children to celebrate each birthday with a party. Adults generally don't have parties each year, but they may have a party for a "big" birthday, such as a 40th or 50th birthday.

THE WEATHER AND SEASONS

A Look at the thermometer. Write a temperature that is:

hot

warm

cool

cold

freezing

B Look at the pictures. Match the pictures to the words.

1. sun
2. rain
3. snow
4. wind
5. clouds

Degrees Fahrenheit	Degrees Celsius	
158	70	
140	60	
122	50	
104	40	
86	30	hot
68	20	warm
50	10	cool
32	0	cold
14	−1	freezing
−4	−20	
−22	−30	
−40	−40	
−58	−50	
−76	−60	

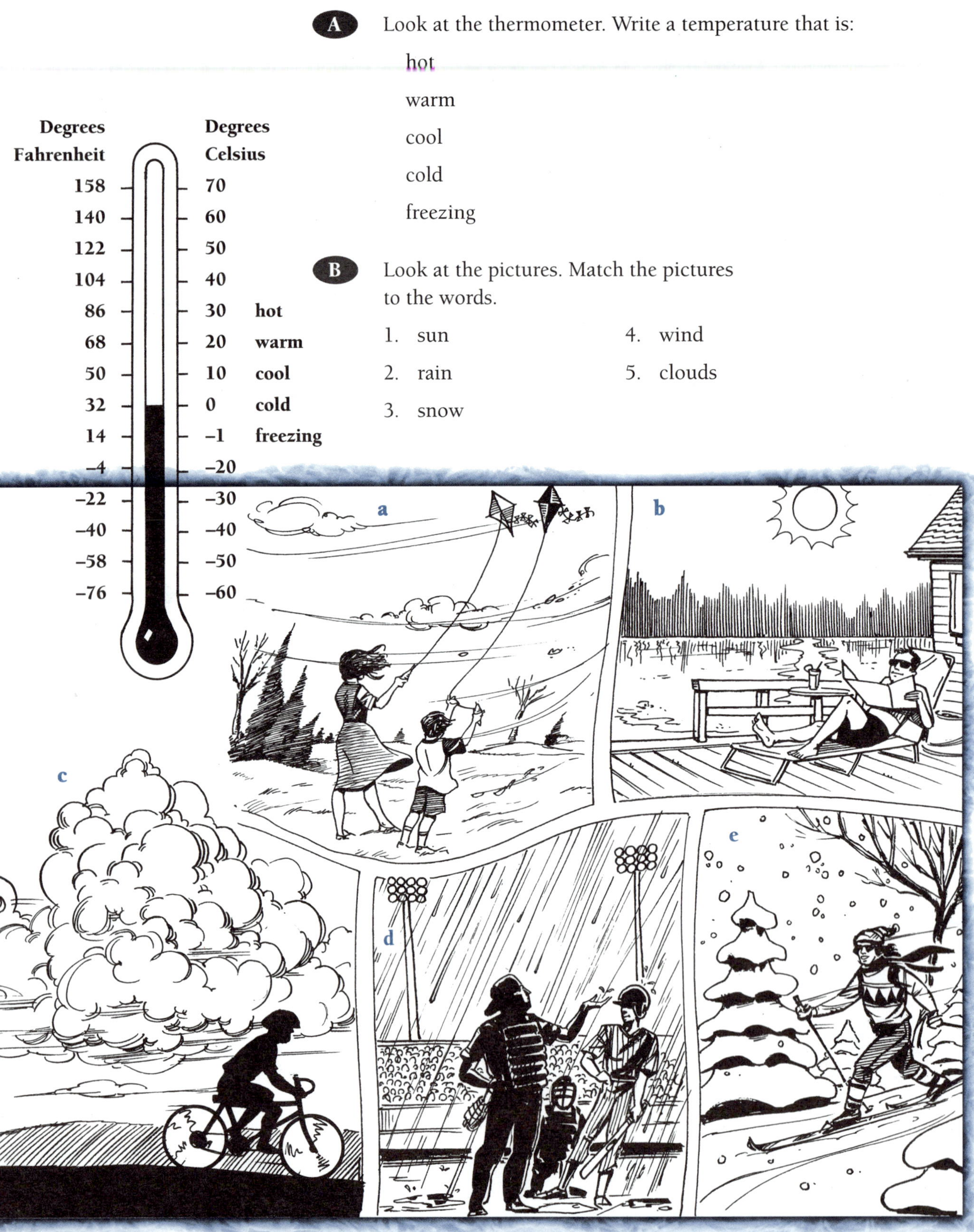

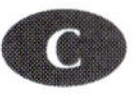

C Look at the pictures of the seasons in Canada. Match the name of the season to the picture.

STOP Use **it is** or **it's** for weather

Say: It is 14 degrees.

It's 0 degrees.

It is minus 15 (–15).

or It's 15 degrees below zero.

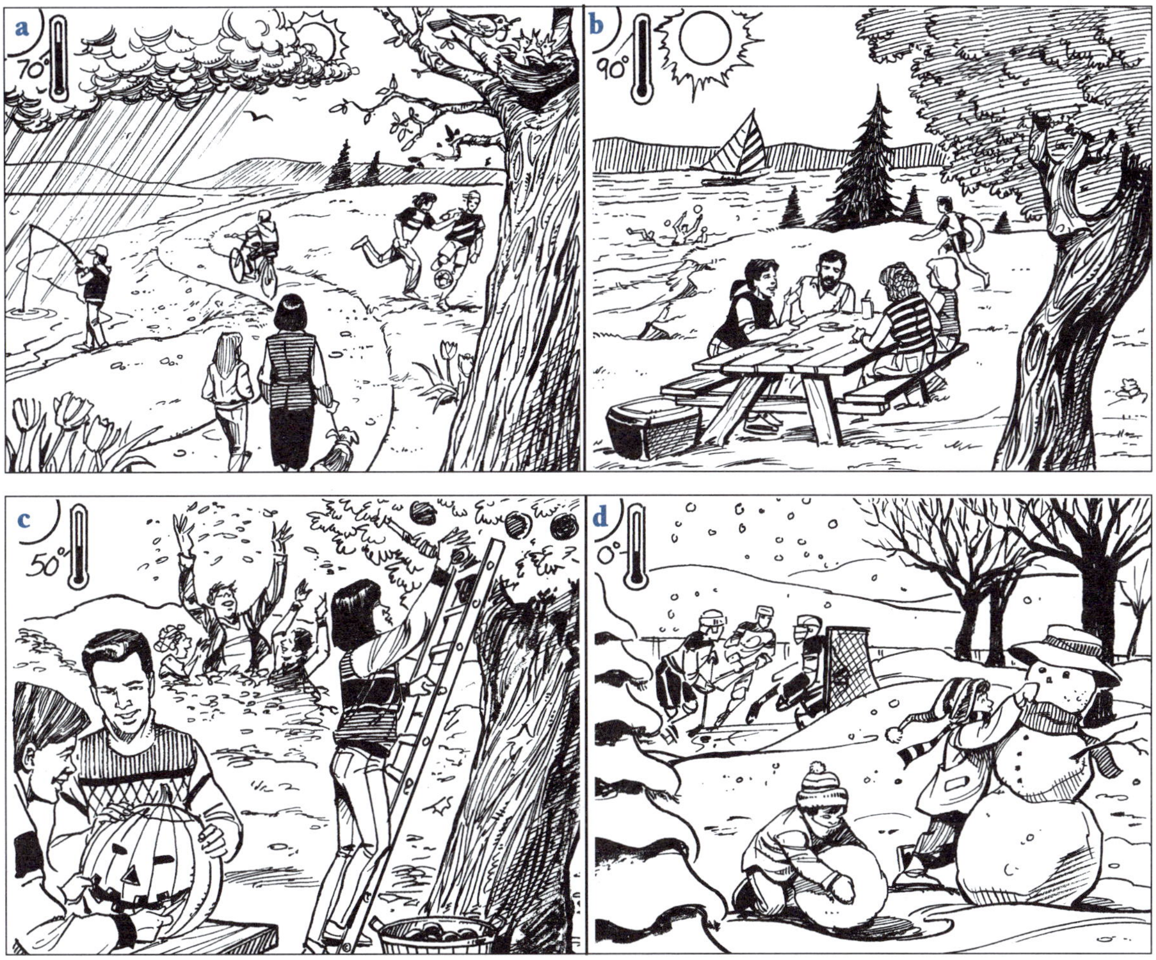

1. winter
2. fall
3. spring
4. summer

D   Look at the charts. Talk with your partner. Answer the questions. Use short answers.

Canada today		
Yellowknife	cloudy	−13
Whitehorse	cloudy	−6
Vancouver	rain	14
Victoria	rain	15
Edmonton	snow	−2
Calgary	cloudy	0
Saskatoon	sunny	−4
Regina	cloudy	1
Winnipeg	snow	3
Toronto	sunny	5
Montreal	rain	4
Fredericton	cloudy	3
Halifax	cloudy	2
Charlottetown	rain	3
St. John's	snow	−4

1. Is it rainy in St. John's?
2. Is it sunny in Toronto?
3. Is Saskatoon hot?
4. Is Fredericton freezing?
5. Is Calgary cloudy?
6. Is Yellowknife warm?
7. Is Regina cold?
8. Is Halifax snowy?
9. Is Charlottetown rainy?
10. Is Vancouver warm?
11. Is Victoria rainy?
12. Is Montreal hot?

WHAT'S THE WEATHER LIKE TODAY?

LISTENING ACTIVITY 4

A   Read the questions with a partner.

B   Listen to Olga call her friend Klara. Answer the questions.

1. Where is Olga?
2. What is the weather like?
3. Where is Klara?
4. What is the weather like?

C   Listen to Jun call his friend Tim. Answer the questions.

1. Where is Jun?

3. Where is Tim?

2. What is the weather like?

4. What is the weather like?

Turn to page 47 for Exercise D.

TALK ABOUT IT

What is the date today? What is the season now?

1. Work in a group. Talk about the weather today. Then talk about the weather in another city or country.

2. Work in pairs. Imagine you are calling a friend in another city. Write a short dialogue about the weather.

"Be": Simple Past

Use the simple past tense for conditions that stopped in past time. Use the forms **was** or **were**. Past-time phrases (**yesterday, this morning, last week**) are sometimes used.

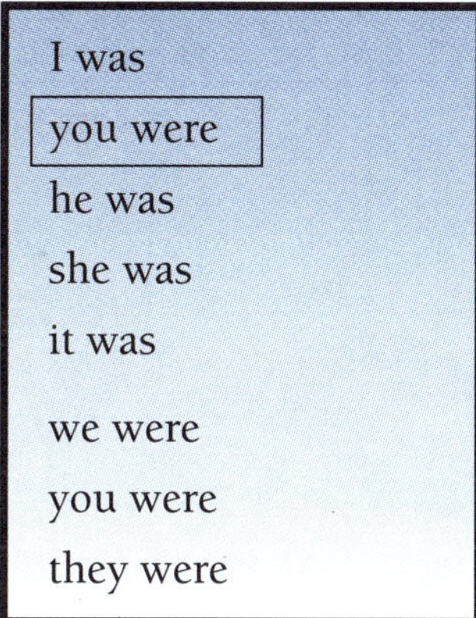

I was

you were

he was

she was

it was

we were

you were

they were

It was hot this morning.

They were late yesterday.

A Answer the questions.

1. Where was Michel yesterday?

2. Where were Olga and Max yesterday?

3. Where was Jun yesterday?

B This morning everyone was busy in the city. Where were these people?
Write sentences about the people.

> Mona was at the dentist.

C   Some verbs are wrong. Find the errors and correct them.

1.   Vancouver were rainy.

2.   The people was happy.

3.   The teacher was Canadian.

4.   The children was excited.

5.   This classroom be old.

6.   The weather were sunny.

7.   Edmonton were freezing.

8.   The books be expensive.

9.   January was cold.

10.   Those women were tired.

"Be": Simple Past Negative

Use **not** after the past form of the verb **be** for negative sentences.

> She **was not** happy yesterday.
>
> They **were not** late this morning.

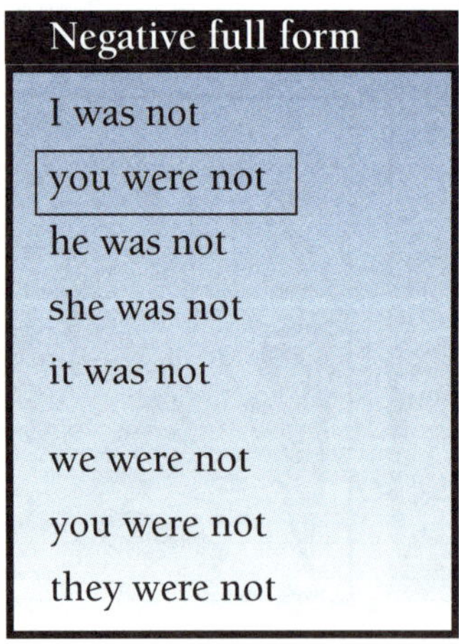

Negative full form
I was not
you were not
he was not
she was not
it was not
we were not
you were not
they were not

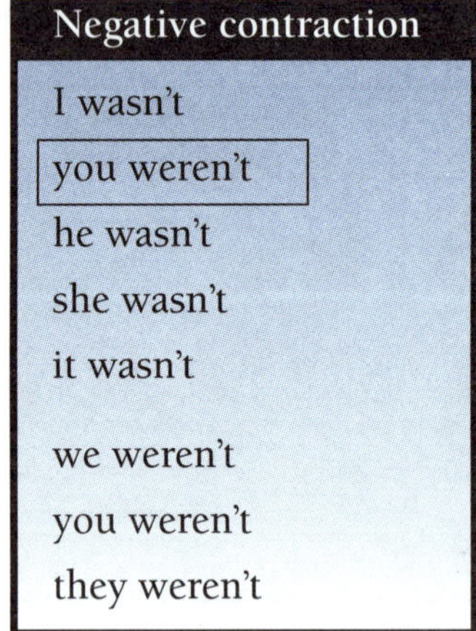

Negative contraction
I wasn't
you weren't
he wasn't
she wasn't
it wasn't
we weren't
you weren't
they weren't

A Write negative sentences. Use contractions.

> He was hungry. **He wasn't hungry.**

1. He was tired.
2. They were late.
3. It was cold yesterday.
4. I was wrong.
5. She was tall.
6. They were Japanese.
7. We were lost.
8. It was at two o'clock.
9. You were happy.
10. She was Canadian.

B Work with a partner. Talk about your last class. Answer the questions with short answers.

1.	Were you in class?	Yes, I was.	No, I wasn't.
2.	Were you early?	Yes, I was.	No, I wasn't.
3.	Was the teacher late?	Yes, he/she was.	No, he/she wasn't.
4.	Was the class hard?	Yes, it was.	No, it wasn't.
5.	Were the students tired?	Yes, they were.	No, they weren't.
6.	Was the weather hot?	Yes, it was.	No it wasn't.
7.	Was your partner hungry?	Yes, he/she was.	No, he/she wasn't.
8.	Was the homework easy?	Yes, it was.	No, it wasn't.
9.	Were you happy?	Yes, I was.	No, I wasn't.
10.	Were the windows open?	Yes, they were.	No, they weren't

GRAMMAR FOCUS — Expressions of Past Time

Use adverbs for showing past time. Adverbs of time are one word (**yesterday**) or a phrase (**on Friday, last night, this morning**). Adverbs of past time answer the question **when**.

Sun	Mon	Tues	Wed	Thurs	Fri	Sat	Sun	Mon	Tues

last Monday   last Tuesday   yesterday   today

 Look at Mona's calendar. Answer the questions.

> When was Mona at the bank?   **last Monday**

Mona's Calendar

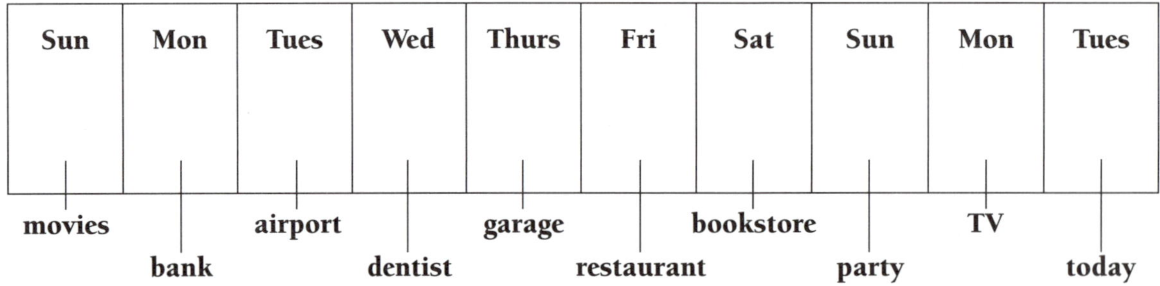

Sun	Mon	Tues	Wed	Thurs	Fri	Sat	Sun	Mon	Tues

movies   airport   garage   bookstore   TV
   bank   dentist   restaurant   party   today

1. When was Mona at the bookstore?
2. When was she at the dentist?
3. When was she at the garage?
4. When was she at the airport?
5. What day were she and her sister at the restaurant?
6. When day was she at home to watch TV?
7. What day was she at the movies?
8. When was she at a party?

WHERE WERE YOU YESTERDAY?

LISTENING ACTIVITY 5

 Look at the pictures. Match the words to the pictures.

  a   b   c   d

1. night   3. evening
2. morning   4. afternoon

  **B**   Read the questions with a partner.

  **C**   Listen and answer the questions. Use the worksheet.

Mona and Olga

1.   Where was Olga in the morning?

2.   When was Olga at the drugstore?

3.   Where was Mona in the morning?

4.   When was Mona at home?

5.   Where was Mona in the evening?

6.   When was Olga at home with her family?

Jun and Carlos

1.   When were Carlos and Ana at the supermarket?

2.   Where were Carlos and Ana in the afternoon?

3.   Where was Jun in the morning?

4.   When was Jun at the post office?

5.   Where was Jun in the evening?

6.   Where were Carlos and Ana in the evening?

Turn to page 47 for Exercise D.

TALK ABOUT IT

Work in a group. Choose a day in the past (yesterday, last Saturday, etc.). Talk about where you were in the morning, in the afternoon, and in the evening.

JOURNAL

 **A**   Read the sentences. Close your book. Listen to the teacher. Write the sentences in your notebook.

> I'm Jun. Last week I was in Toronto. The weather was warm and sunny. I was at movies, restaurants, and stores. I was at the CN Tower on Saturday. I was very happy.

  **B**   Where were you last week? Write five sentences about you.

Categories

Put these words in groups. There are six groups, with three words each.

afternoon	September
bank	snow
evening	spring
hospital	summer
July	sun
Monday	Sunday
morning	supermarket
October	Wednesday
rain	winter

Find Someone

Walk around the room and ask questions to find people who were in the places on the list. When a student answers "yes," write his or her name. The first person to finish is the winner.

Ask: Were you…?

Answer: Yes, I was. No, I wasn't.

Find someone who:

1. was at home last night
2. was in a restaurant last weekend
3. was in class last Thursday
4. was in a bank yesterday
5. was in a supermarket yesterday afternoon
6. was in a store last Saturday
7   was at a party last weekend
8. was at the movies last night
9. was at the dentist last month
10. was in the library yesterday
11. was at home yesterday morning
12. was at a drugstore last week

WHAT'S THE WEATHER LIKE TODAY?

LISTENING ACTIVITY 4

  **D**   Practise the conversations with a partner.

Klara and Olga

Olga: Hi, Klara. How are you?

Klara: I'm OK, Olga. How's Vancouver?

Olga: Vancouver is great, but it's a little rainy.

Klara: Well, it's snowing here in Halifax.

Olga: That's too bad. Well, call me soon.

Klara: I will. Goodbye.

Olga: 'Bye.

Tim and Jun

Jun: Hi, Tim. How are you?

Tim   I'm fine, Jun. How's Toronto?

Jun: Toronto's great. It's sunny and warm today.

Tim: You're lucky. It's freezing here in Winnipeg.

Jun: That's too bad.

Tim: 'Bye.

WHERE WERE YOU YESTERDAY?

LISTENING ACTIVITY 5

  **D**   Listen and write the words. Use the worksheet.

Mona and Olga

Mona: Where __________ you yesterday, Olga?

Olga: I __________ at home in the morning, Mona. I was __________ the drugstore in the afternoon. What about you?

Mona: I was __________ the bank in the morning. I __________ at home in the afternoon.

Olga: Where ___________ you in the evening?

Mona: I was __________ a restaurant with my friend. What about you?

Olga: I __________ at home with my family yesterday evening.

Jun and Carlos

Jun: Hi, Carlos. Where ___________ you yesterday?

Carlos: In the morning, I ___________ at the supermarket with Ana. In the afternoon, we __________ at the movies. What about you?

Jun: I __________ busy yesterday too. In __________ morning I was at __________ dentist. In the afternoon I was at the post office.

Carlos: Where ___________ you in the evening?

Jun: I __________ at a party. What about you?

Carlos: Ana and I __________ at home.

E   Practise the conversations with a partner.

BIRTHDAYS

Partner B

1.   Work with another "Partner B." Write the ages for the people on the left side of the chart.

2.   Then work with a "Partner A" to find the ages of the people on the right. Give your partner information about the names on the left.

   Ask: How old is Tara?

   Answer: Mark is ________ years old.

	Date of birth			Age		Age
	Day	Month	Year			
Mark	09	10	1988	______	Tara	______
Milly	27	05	1926	______	John	______
Scott	25	01	1984	______	Ralph	______
Melanie	11	04	1982	______	Rick	______
Lisa	21	12	1954	______	Julia	______
Kelly	15	02	1977	______	Andrea	______
Bruce	28	11	1959	______	Miriam	______

UNIT 4

FAMILY AND FRIENDS

OLGA'S FAMILY

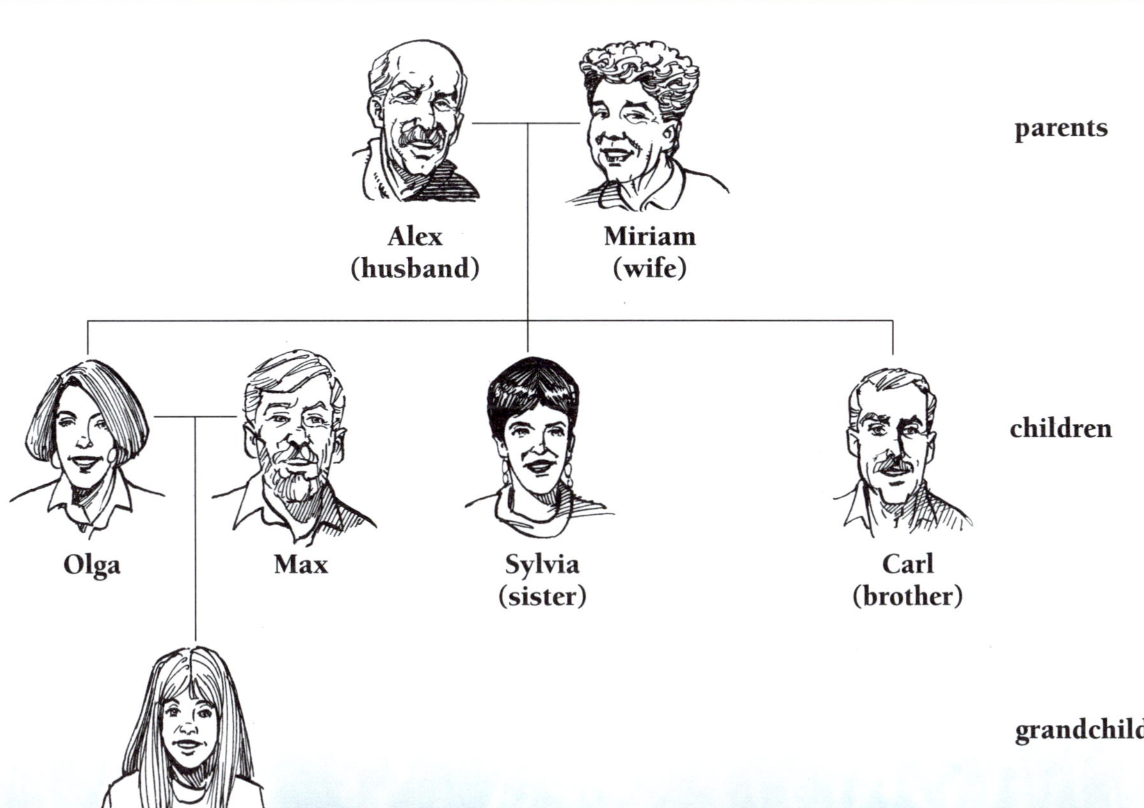

A   Look at the family tree.

B   Read the sentences with a partner. Answer "yes" or "no."

1. Max and Olga are husband and wife.

2. Carl and Sylvia are brothers.

3. Masha is Sylvia's sister.

4. Masha is Alex and Miriam's grandchild.

5. Olga and Sylvia are sisters.

6. Max and Alex are brothers.

7. Carl is a parent.

8. Max and Olga are parents.

Possessive Nouns

Add apostrophe **s** ('**s**) to nouns to show possession. Use this form for people's names or job titles.

> Joseph's sister
>
> the teacher's desk

A   Write the possessive form of the nouns.

> sister/Michele   **Michele's sister**

1. brother/Anne
2. friend/Susan
3. sister/George
4. grandmother/Mona
5. brother/Lisa
6. husband/the teacher
7. wife/Henry
8. mother/David
9. father/Carla
10. grandfather/Steve

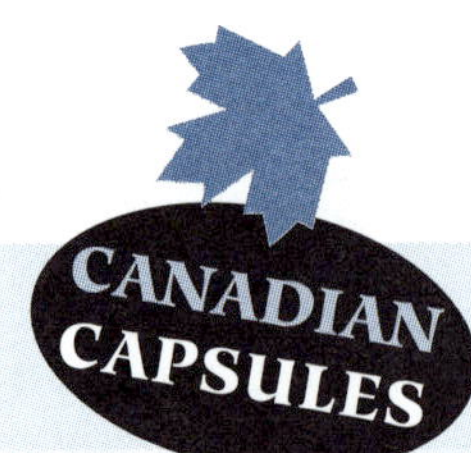

In some parts of the world, families are big. In Canada, most families are small. It is common to have one, two, or three children.

KATE'S FAMILY TREE

A Look at Kate's family tree. Work with a partner to answer the questions.

1. How many people are in the family?

2. How many adults are in the family?

3. How many children are in the family?

4. How many people are male?

5. How many people are female?

6. How many people are parents?

7. How many people are grandparents?

B Work with a partner. Answer the questions. Write the names of the people.

1. Who are Kate's parents?

2. Who is Michael's wife?

3. Who are Anne's daughters?

4. Who is Susan's son?

5. Who are Tara's aunts?

6. Who is Susan's nephew?

7. Who are David's sisters?

8. Who is Robert's uncle?

9. Who are John's granddaughters?

10. Who is Andrea's sister?

11. Who is Johanne's mother?

12. Who is Joseph's father?

13. Who are Kate's nieces?

14. Who is Maria's husband?

WHAT A NICE FAMILY

LISTENING ACTIVITY 6

A   Read the questions with a partner.

B   Listen and complete the sentences.

Jun and Michel

1. Pierre is Michel's ________________.

2. Pierre is ________________ years old.

3. Lise is Michel's ________________.

4. Lise is ________________ years old.

Kate and Mona

1. Mona has ________________ uncles and ________________ aunts.

2. She has ________________ cousins.

3. Mona has ________________ brother.

Turn to page 59 for Exercise C.

MY FAMILY

Draw your family tree. Draw and label you, your grandparents, your parents, sisters and brothers, aunts and uncles, and cousins.

TALK ABOUT IT

Show your family tree to your group. Talk about your family.

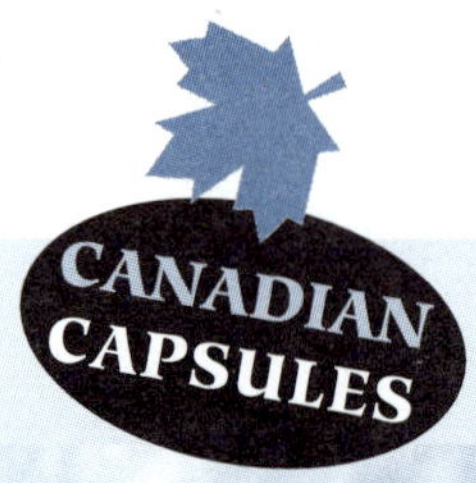

CANADIAN CAPSULES

When people in Canada finish high school or college, they often live alone for a while before they get married.

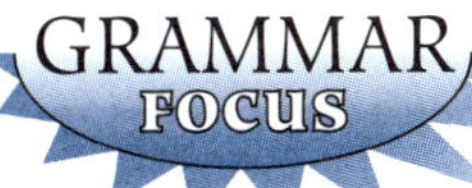

GRAMMAR FOCUS

Possessive Adjectives

Possessive adjectives show **who** owns something. Use possessive adjectives before nouns.

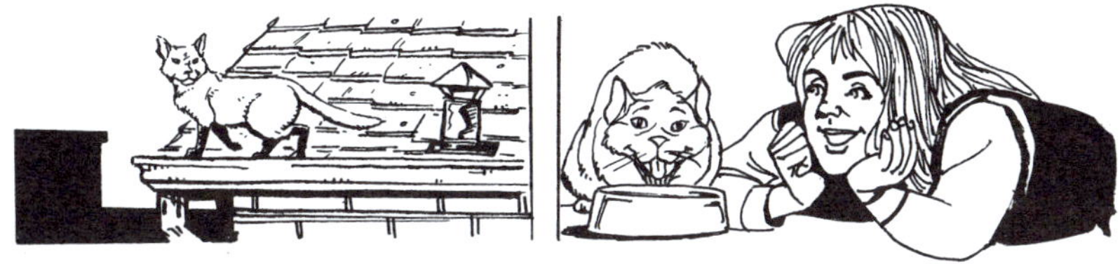

not **a** cat (general) but **my** cat (possession)

Subject pronouns	Possessive adjectives
I	my
you	your
he	his
she	her
it	its
we	our
you	your
they	their

A Put the possessive adjectives in the paragraph. Use each word once.

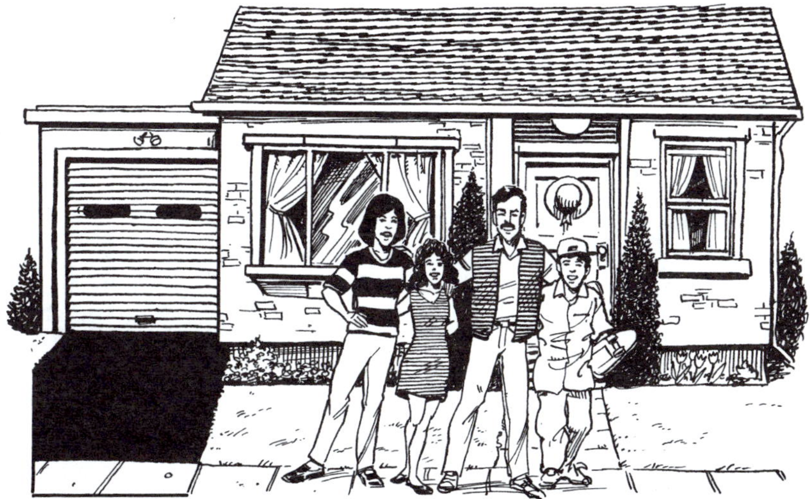

her **their** **his** **his** **her**

This is the Di Allo family. They are near ___________ house. Tony Di Allo is between ___________ son and ___________ daughter. Maria is between ___________ father and ___________ mother.

B   Put the possessive adjectives in the letter. Use each word once.

my   our   our   my   our   your

Dear Nicole,

This is my family. We are near __________ house. I am near __________ mother, Denise. That is __________ father, Robert. Paul is my little brother. He is near __________ father. Melanie is my older sister. She is near __________ brother. Please send a picture of __________ family.

Your friend,

Julie

PEOPLE AROUND YOU

A Read about the people in the class. Write the name for each person.

1. She is a woman. She has short blond hair and blue eyes. She is medium height. She is 28 years old. She is Canadian. She is ____________.

2. She has long black hair. She is not tall. She is short. She is from China. She is 31 years old. She is ____________.

3. He is tall and thin. He has black hair and brown eyes. He has a beard and a moustache. He is from Haiti. He is 25 years old. He is ____________.

4. She is medium height. She has brown hair and brown eyes. She is married. She is ____________. Her husband has a beard and moustache. He is ____________.

5. He is Korean. He is 24 years old. He has straight black hair. He is not tall, but he is not short. He is medium height. He has glasses. He is ______________.

6. She is 21 years old. She has long, curly dark hair. She is from Egypt. She has glasses. She is a nurse. She is ______________.

7. They are married. The woman is 33 years old. She is medium height. She has dark hair. The man is 35 years old. He has a moustache. He also has glasses. They are ______________ and ______________.

ARE THESE YOUR FRIENDS?

LISTENING ACTIVITY 7

Lili and Ana are looking at pictures.

    **A**   Read the sentences with a partner.

    **B**   Listen and answer "yes" or "no."

Lili's Friends

1. Lili's friends are from Halifax.

2. The tall girl has long hair.

3. Laurie has short hair.

Ana's Friends

1. Ana's friends are from Calgary.

2. Ted is thin.

3. Ted has glasses.

4. Sue is Ted's sister.

5. Their daughter has blond hair.

6. Their son has brown hair.

Turn to page 60 for Exercise C.

Think about a person you know: a friend or someone in your family. Talk about the person. What does he or she look like? Your group will try to guess who the person is.

JOURNAL

A   Read the sentences. Close your book. Listen to the teacher. Write the sentences in your notebook.

> I'm Mona. My mother is Nadia. My father is Omar. I have a brother. His name is Ali.

> My father is tall. He has glasses. My mother is medium height. She has brown hair.

B   Write about your family.

TEN-MINUTE GAMES AND ACTIVITIES

Opposites

Match the opposites in Box A and Box B.

Box A

mother   husband
brother   children
young   tall
happy
married   boy
son   small
grandmother
heavy
uncle   female
man   nephew

Box B

sad
aunt   woman
parents   single
short   old
sister
girl   niece
male
grandfather   big   thin
wife
father   daughter

Family Members

Work in pairs to complete the puzzle.

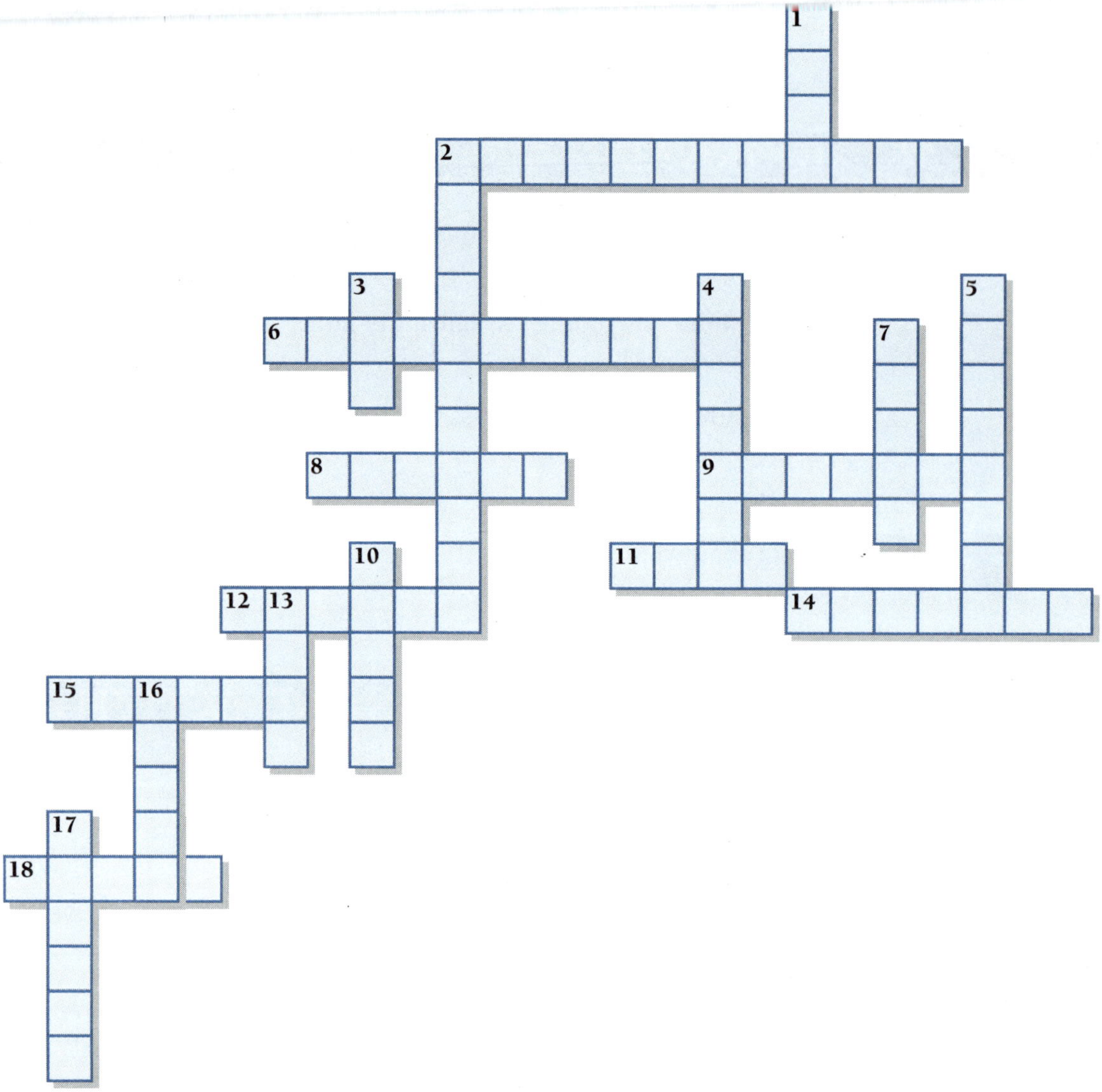

Across

2. Your mother's parents are your ____________.

6. Your mother's mother is your ____________.

8. There are three children in your family. You have a brother and a ____________.

9. If you are a married woman, you have a ____________.

11. A young female is called a ____________.

12. Your parents are your mother and your ____________.

14. Your mother and father are your ____________.

15. Your aunt and uncle's child is your ____________.

18. Adult females are called ____________.

Down

1. If you are a married man, you have a ____________.

2. The father of your mother or father is your ____________.

3. The opposite of "woman" is ____________.

4. If there is another child in your family, and you don't have a sister, you have a ____________.

5. The plural of "child" is ____________.

7. Your mother is a ____________.

10. A young person is called a ____________.

13. Your mother's sister is your ____________.

16. The brother of your father or mother is your ____________.

17. Your parents are your father and ____________.

WHAT A NICE FAMILY

Practise the conversations with a partner.

Jun and Michel

Jun: Is this your family, Michel?

Michel: Yes, it is.

Jun: Who's this?

Michel: That's my brother Pierre.

Jun: How old is he?

Michel: He's 11 years old.

Jun: And who is the girl next to you?

Michel: Oh, that's my sister, Lise. She's 9 year's old.

Kate and Mona

Kate: Is this your family, Mona?

Mona: Yes, it is. I have a big family.

Kate: How many uncles and aunts do you have?

Mona: I have four uncles and five aunts.

Kate: And how many cousins do you have?

Mona: I have 15 cousins.

Kate: Do you have any brothers or sisters?

Mona: Yes, I have one brother, named Ali.

ARE THESE YOUR FRIENDS?

LISTENING ACTIVITY 7

  **C**   Listen and write the words. Use the worksheet.

Lili's Friends

Ana: Who are these people, Lili?

Lili: These are ______________ friends from Vancouver, Ana.

Ana: Who is ______________ tall girl with long hair?

Lili: ______________ my friend Kelly.

Ana: And who's the girl ______________ short hair?

Lili: That's ______________ sister Laurie.

Ana's Friends

Lili: Who are ______________ people, Ana?

Ana: Those are ______________ friends from Calgary, Ted and Sue.

Lili: ______________ Ted the heavy man with the glasses?

Ana: Yes ______________ is. Sue is ______________ wife.

Lili: Who ______________ the children in the picture?

Ana: The girl with blond hair is ______________ daughter. The boy ______________ brown hair is their son.

  **D**   Practise the conversations with a partner.

TELLING TIME

 **A** Practise with the teacher. Look at the clocks. Listen and repeat.

> | Questions: | What time is it? |
> | | Can you please tell me the time? |
> | Answers: | It's 6:15 (six fifteen). |
> | | It's 4:30 (four thirty). |

 **STOP** Use **It is** or **It's** for time.

4:00
It's four o'clock

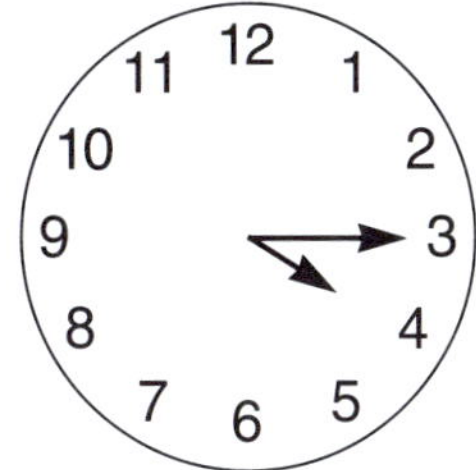

4:15
It's four fifteen
OR a quarter past four.

4:30
It's four thirty
OR half past four.

4:45
It's four forty-five
OR a quarter to five.

B   Circle the times that your teacher says. Use the worksheet.

1. a) 2:40
    b) 2:45
    c) 1:11

2. a) 3:15
    b) 3:50
    c) 3:55

3. a) 6:12
    b) 6:20
    c) 6:25

4. a) 9:05
    b) 9:50
    c) 9:15

5. a) 5:55
    b) 5:35
    c) 5:05

6. a) 11:10
    b) 11:11
    c) 11:31

7. a) 4:25
    b) 4:20
    c) 2:40

8. a) 6:30
    b) 6:35
    c) 6:25

9. a) 7:55
    b) 7:15
    c) 7:45

10. a) 1:10
    b) 1:12
    c) 10:10

C   Practise with a partner. Say the times.

| 6:05   Say: **six-o-five** |

3:15	12:00	4:40	1:05
8:25	11:05	6:30	9:20
2:45	5:50	7:10	10:35

D   Write the times on the clocks. Use the worksheet.

E   Write the times the teacher says. Use your notebook.

IN THE MORNING

A   Read the sentences about Lili. Match the sentences with the pictures.

1. Lili wakes up.
2. She gets up.
3. She washes her face.
4. She gets dressed.
5. She brushes her hair.
6. She eats breakfast.
7. She brushes her teeth.
8. She drives to school.
9. Class starts at 9:00.

B   Read the Story

In the Morning

Lili wakes up at 7 o'clock. She gets up and brushes her teeth. Then she washes her face and brushes her hair. Next, she gets dressed. At 7:30 Lili has breakfast. At 8:00 Lili goes to school. She drives her car. It takes a long time. There are many cars on the road. English class starts at 9:00.

C   Work with a partner. Answer the questions. Say "yes" or "no."

1. Lili wakes up at 8 o'clock.

2. Lili brushes her teeth first.

3. Lili gets dressed before she washes her face.

4. Lili has breakfast at 7:30.

5. Lili goes to school at 8:30.

6. Lili takes the bus to school.

7. Class starts at 9:00.

D   Read the story again. Put the pictures on page 63 in order.

> 1. **e**

TALK ABOUT IT

1. Talk with your partner. Tell the story about Lili in the morning. Use the pictures to help you.

2. Talk about you. Tell your partner about your morning routine.

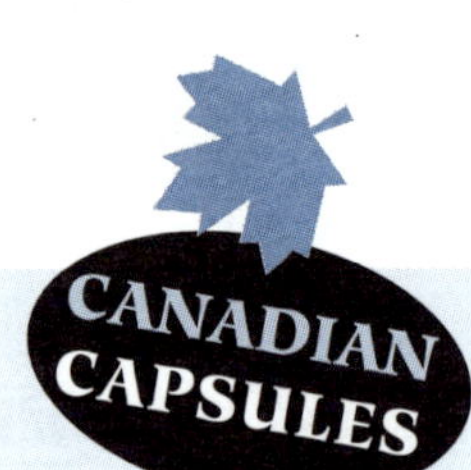

In Vancouver, many people go to work by bus, but some people go to work by sea-bus. They can take a transfer and change from the sea-bus to the city bus.

Present Simple Tense

Use the present simple to describe things that don't change or actions that are habitual.

> The sun rises every day.
>
> I wake up at seven o'clock.

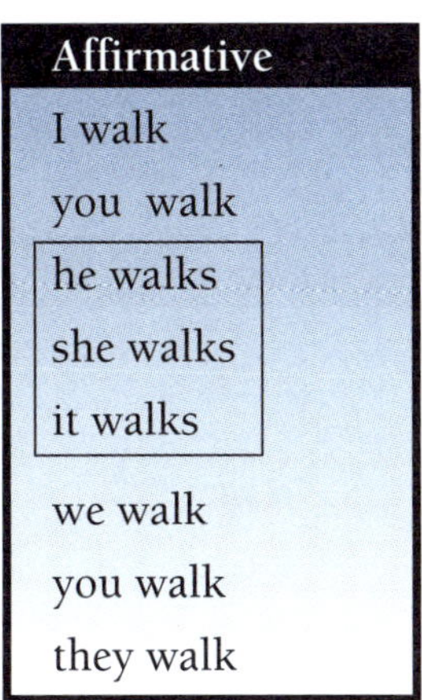

Affirmative

I walk

you walk

he walks

she walks

it walks

we walk

you walk

they walk

Use the base form of the verb for the present simple tense. Add **s** or **es** to the base form with **he**, **she**, and **it**.

> I walk to school.   She walk**s** to school.
>
> I go to school.   She go**es** to school.

A   Complete the sentences. Use the correct form of the verb in brackets.

1.   Lili and Amy _______________ tea for breakfast. (drink)

2.   Mona usually _______________ before seven o'clock. (wake up)

3.   He _______________ in a hospital. (work)

4.   Joseph and Tim _______________ to school. (walk)

5.   People in Toronto often _______________ to work. (drive)

6.   Maria _______________ eggs and toast for breakfast. (eat)

7.   Carlos and Ana _______________ TV in the evening. (watch)

8.   Jun _______________ the bus to work. (take)

9.   He _______________ home with his friend. (walk)

10.   We _______________ to sleep early. (go)

B   Choose the verb. Use the correct form.

go   leave   work   eat   watch   take   study   get up   finish

Michel is a student. He **1**__________ every day. He **2**__________ early and **3**__________ breakfast. He **4**__________ for class at eight o'clock. He **5**__________ the bus to school.

Michel also has a part-time job. After school he **6**__________ in a restaurant. He **7**__________ at 9:15. Then he **8**__________ home. At home, he **9**__________ TV.

COMING TO CLASS

A   Look at the picture. Find:

a bus   a car
a subway station   a taxi

B   Read the story.

Coming to Class

The students come to class in different ways. Olga and Max live near the school. They walk from their apartment. They can walk to class in about 10 minutes.

Kate's apartment is not near the class. She drives to class every day. It takes about 20 minutes to drive there. Kate parks her car on the street near the school building.

Lili lives at her aunt and uncle's house. She travels to class by subway. The subway takes about 35 minutes.

Mona's family lives a short distance from the school. Their apartment is near the bus stop. It takes Mona 15 minutes to come to school by bus.

C   Copy the chart in your notebook. Write the information in the chart.

	Olga and Max	Kate	Lili	Mona
The way they come to school	walk			
The time it takes				

TALK ABOUT IT

Walk around the classroom. Talk to six students. Talk about how you come to class and how long it takes. Ask other students about coming to class.

Ask: How do you come to class?   **Say:** I…

How long does it take?   It takes…

In cold cities, such as Toronto and Montreal, people use the subway to stay warm underground. In Montreal, the subway is called the "Metro."

SURVEY: TRANSPORTATION

Copy the chart. Walk around the class. Talk to six different students. Ask how they come to class.

Name	How he/she comes to class	Time it takes
1.		
2.		
3.		
4.		
5.		
6.		

HOW TO TAKE A BUS

A Work with a partner. Match the pictures to the sentences on page 69.

B   Put the pictures in order.

1. Look for a bus stop.

2. Sit down on a seat.

3. Put the ticket or money in the fare box.

4. Watch for your stop.

5. Get a transfer from the driver.

6. Pull the cord to ring the bell.

7. Get into the bus.

8. Get off the bus.

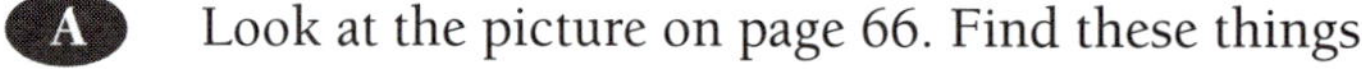

HOW DO I GET THERE?

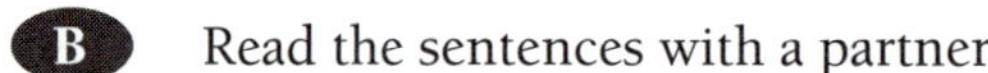
LISTENING ACTIVITY 8

A Look at the picture on page 66. Find these things:

1. a bus stop
2. traffic lights
3. a corner
4. a mailbox
5. a crosswalk
6. a fire hydrant
7. a stop sign

B Read the sentences with a partner.

C Listen to Michel give directions. Write "yes" or "no."

Conversation 1

1. The woman wants to find the bus stop.
2. The subway station is near the traffic lights.

Conversation 2

1. The man wants to go downtown.
2. The Number 95 bus goes downtown.
3. The bus stop is beside the mailbox.

Turn to page 75 for Exercise D.

TALK ABOUT IT

Work in a group. Talk about how to go to your house by bus or subway. Where do you get the bus? Where do you get on and off?

IN THE EVENING

A   Look at the pictures. Match the sentences with the pictures.

1. Olga cooks supper.
2. English class finishes at noon.
3. The family eats supper.
4. Masha goes to bed.
5. Max washes the dishes.

6. Olga and Max go to sleep.
7. Olga and Max watch TV.
8. Masha takes a bath.
9. Max takes Masha home from school.
10. Masha does her homework.

B Read the story. Then put the pictures in order.

In the Evening

The English class finishes at noon. Olga goes home. Max works. He drives a taxi until 5 o'clock. At 5:30 he goes to Masha's school. He takes his daughter home.

Olga cooks supper for the family. They eat supper at 6:30. After supper Max washes the dishes. Masha does her homework. Then she takes a bath. Masha goes to bed at 8:30. Olga and Max watch television in the living room. They go to sleep at 10:30.

C Look at the clocks. Match the times to the things Max, Olga and Masha do.

a
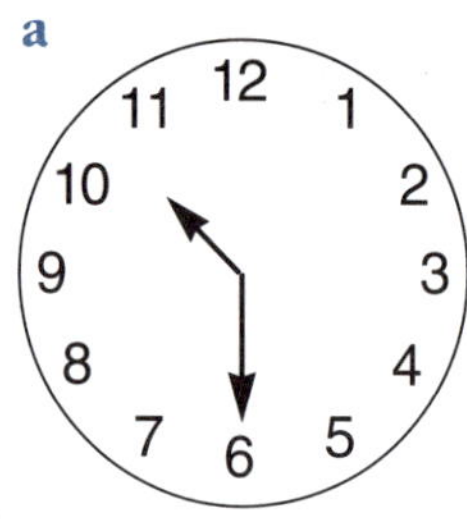

b
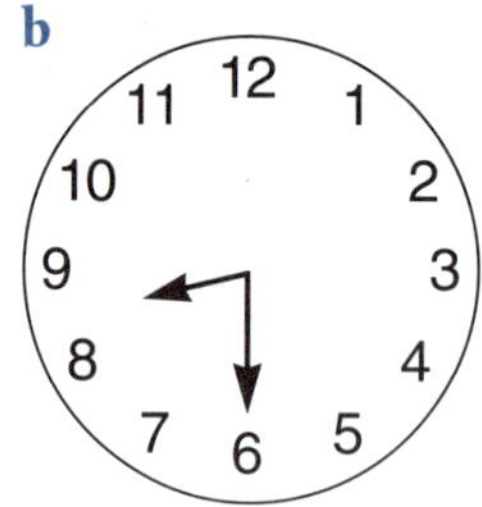

c
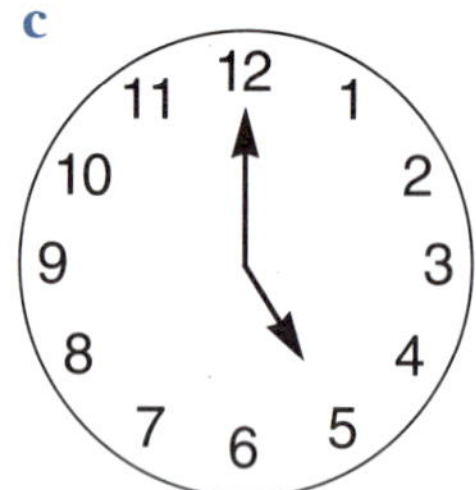

d
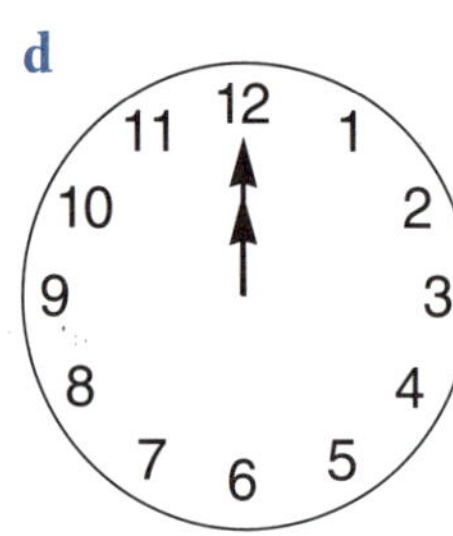

e
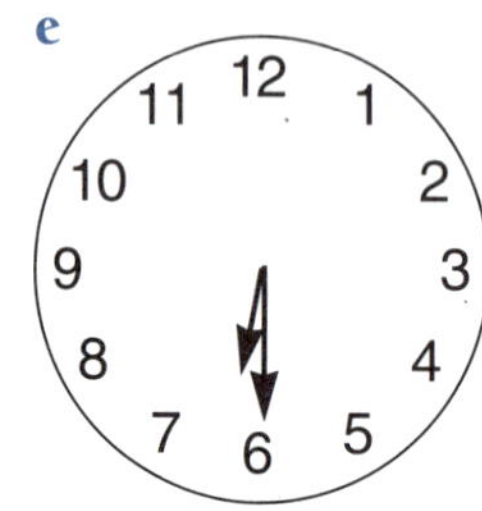

f
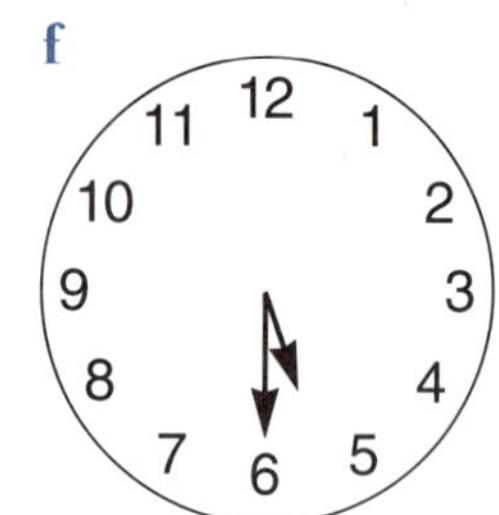

1. **b**

1. Masha goes to bed.
2. Max finishes work.
3. The English class finishes.
4. Max and Olga go to sleep.
5. They eat supper.
6. Max picks up Masha at school.

TALK ABOUT IT

1. Talk about Max and Olga's evening routine. Use the pictures to help you.
2. Talk about your evening routine.

MAKING AN APPOINTMENT

LISTENING ACTIVITY **9**

A   Look at the pictures. Who are Jun and Olga calling?

   **B**   Read the questions with your partner.

   **C**   Listen and answer the questions. Write "yes" or "no."

Jun's Appointment

1. Jun calls a doctor's office.
2. Jun is busy on Wednesday.
3. Jun can come in on Thursday.
4. The appointment is at 11:30.

Olga's Appointment

1. Olga wants to make an appointment.
2. Olga can come in at 10:00.
3. Olga can come in at 2:00.
4. The appointment is for Friday.

Turn to page 76 for Exercise D.

TALK ABOUT IT

Work with a partner. Write a new conversation about making an appointment.

JOURNAL

 **A**   Read the sentences. Close your book. Listen to the teacher. Write the sentences in your notebook.

> I'm Lili. I go to English class every morning. I work in the bank in the afternoons. I go home at 5:30. I cook supper at 6:00. In the evening I watch TV and read.

  **B**   Write about your daily routine. What do you do in the morning? In the afternoon? In the evening?

TEN-MINUTE GAMES AND ACTIVITIES

Find Someone

Walk around the room. Ask other students questions about their daily habits. When a student answers "yes," write his or her name. The first person to finish is the winner.

Ask: Do you…?

Answer: Yes, I do.   No, I don't.

Find someone who:

1. eats a big breakfast every morning
2. drinks coffee in the evening
3. drinks tea
4. takes the bus to class
5. wakes up early on Saturdays
6. eats lunch in a restaurant
7. goes to sleep late every day
8. drives to class
9. lives with friends
10. speaks Greek
11. cooks supper every day
12. watches TV in the afternoon
13. plays the piano
14. speaks Spanish
15. reads the newspaper in the evening

Game: Everyday Tic-Tac-Toe

Students work in two teams: Team **X** and Team **O**.

A student from Team **X** begins by choosing a verb from the grid below, and making a sentence about something he or she does every day.

> I travel to school by bus.
>
> I do my homework in the evening.

If the student uses the verb correctly, the teacher marks an **X** on the matching square on a grid on the board.

A student from Team **O** selects a square and makes a sentence in the same way. If the student uses the verb correctly, the teacher marks an **O** in the square.

The first team to get three **X**s or three **O**s in a row wins. The rows can be vertical, horizontal or diagonal.

1.

walk	**eat**	**travel**
cook	**take**	**watch**
listen	**wash**	**do**

2.

go	**leave**	**work**
read	**wake up**	**study**
leave	**live**	**finish**

HOW DO I GET THERE?

LISTENING ACTIVITY 8

  **D**   Practise the conversations with a partner.

Conversation 1

Woman: Excuse me. Where is the subway station?

Michel: It's across the street. It's right near the traffic lights.

Woman: Near the traffic lights? OK. Thank you.

Michel: You're welcome.

Conversation 2

Man: Excuse me. I'm lost. I want to go downtown. Where is the bus stop?

Michel: The 92 bus goes downtown. The bus stop is at the corner.

Man: At the corner? Is the bus stop across the street?

Michel: Yes. Cross the street at the crosswalk. It's right beside the mailbox.

Man: Thank you.

Michel: You're welcome.

MAKING AN APPOINTMENT

D   Listen and write the words. Use the worksheet.

Jun's Appointment

Receptionist: Hello, Dr. Scott's office. Can I help ___________?

Jun: Yes, I'd like to make ___________ appointment please.

Receptionist: Can you come in ___________ Wednesday, at 11:00?

Jun: No, I'm sorry, I can't. I'm busy on Wednesday.

Receptionist: ___________ OK. Can you come in on Thursday ___________ 10:30?

Jun: Yes, I can.

Receptionist: OK, we'll see you _________ Thursday _________ 10:30.

Olga's Appointment

Receptionist: Hello, Dr. Scott's office. Can I ___________ you?

Olga: Yes. I'd like ___________ make an appointment please.

Receptionist: Can you come ___________ tomorrow ___________10:00?

Olga: No, I can't. I'm busy ___________ 10:00.

Receptionist: How about at 2:00?

Olga: Yes, _______________ fine.

Receptionist: OK, that's Tuesday at 2:00. See _______________ then.

E   Practise the conversations with a partner.

THE FOOD QUIZ

 **A** Work with a partner. Find the word that is different in each line.

> mushrooms peppers milk celery **milk**

1. onions potatoes carrots beef

2. apples eggs oranges bananas

3. beef ham chicken grapes

4. milk cookies coffee tea

5. cheese tomato yogurt ice cream

6. bread chops cereal cookies

7. carrots pepper noodles corn

8. cucumber fish lobster shrimp

B Look at the pictures. Practise saying the foods with the teacher.

C   Work with a partner. Look at the picture on page 78. Write the names of:

1.   three kinds of fruit
2.   two foods that are orange
3.   three kinds of meat
4.   three foods that you eat cold
5.   three foods that are red
6.   three foods you eat with a spoon
7.   three foods you eat for supper
8.   two foods that you eat for dessert
9.   three things you drink
10.   three foods that are white
11.   three foods that you eat with a fork and knife
12.   three foods people eat for breakfast
13.   three foods that you eat hot
14.   three foods that are yellow
15.   three foods that we put in a salad
16.   four foods that begin with the letter C
17.   three foods that are green
18.   two things we put in coffee

TALK ABOUT IT

1.   Look at the pictures again. Make a list of foods you like.
2.   Walk around the classroom. Talk to six students about foods you like and foods you don't like.

     Ask: Do you like...?

     Say: I like...

     I don't like...

SURVEY: FOOD FAVOURITES

Copy the chart. Walk around the classroom. Talk to five other students.
Ask about five foods they like. Write the foods in the chart.

Name:					
Foods:					
1.					
2.					
3.					
4.					
5.					

Present Simple Tense: Negative

Use **do not** before the verb.

Use **does not** before the verb with **he**, **she**, and **it**.

I **do not** live here.

He **does not** live here.

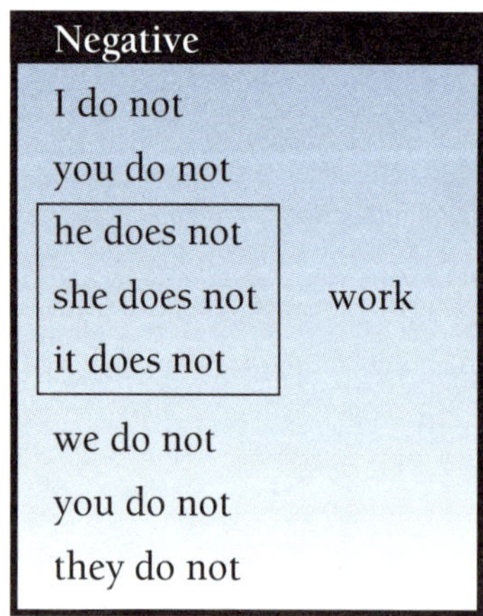

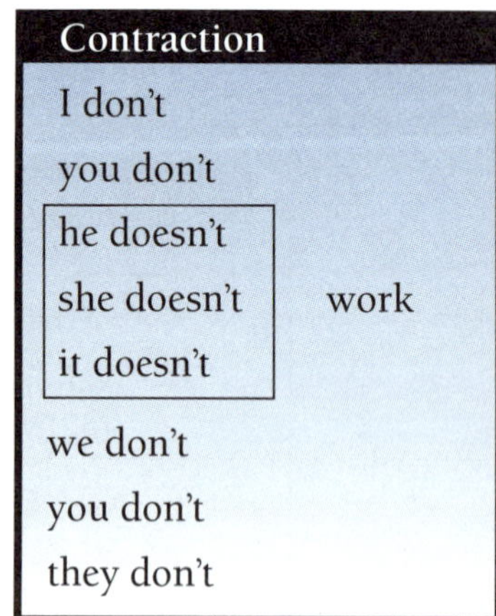

He **works**, but he **does** not **work**.

A Write the sentences in the negative. Use contractions.

> I like cookies.   **I don't like** cookies.

1. Students get up late.
2. Juan and Michel take pictures.
3. They eat dinner at home.
4. He writes letters to his parents.
5. We stay home in the evening.
6. She buys food at the supermarket.
7. Julie shops at the corner store.
8. We eat breakfast in the cafeteria.
9. She makes lunch every day.
10. Annie drinks tea in the morning.

B Some sentences are wrong. Find the errors and correct them.

1. James doesn't take the bus to school.
2. Carla doesn't eats in the cafeteria often.
3. Lise and Patricia don't walks to work.
4. Dina don't go to bed early.
5. Maria doesn't cook dinner on Sundays.
6. We doesn't speak Spanish.
7. He doesn't watch TV in the evening.
8. They doesn't eat rice for breakfast.
9. She doesn't drink coffee every morning.
10. I doesn't work in a restaurant.

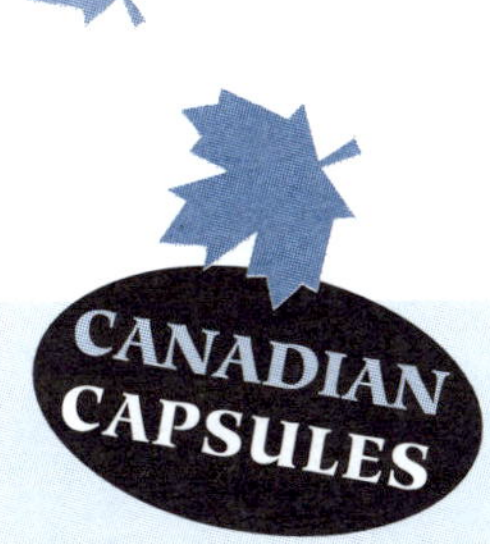

CANADIAN CAPSULES

Most people in Canada eat three meals a day. Breakfast is in the morning; lunch is around noon (12:00 p.m.); and supper, which is sometimes called dinner, is at about six or seven o'clock.

A SHOPPING LIST

LISTENING ACTIVITY 10

  **A** Look at the shopping lists. Listen to the conversations. Find the shopping lists for these people:

1. Ana and Carlos

2. Max and Olga

3. Jun and Tim

Turn to page 90 for Exercise B.

TALK ABOUT IT

Work with a partner.

1. Make a shopping list.
2. Write a new conversation about shopping for groceries.

A Look at the picture. Name the foods that you see.

B Read the story.

A Family Restaurant

Nick's family has a restaurant. The restaurant serves many different kinds of food.

The whole family works in the restaurant. Nick's uncle and aunt cook the food. His cousin George is a waiter. He serves the food. On Saturdays and Sundays, Nick helps his cousin serve the food.

On the weekends the restaurant is very busy. The kitchen is warm. Everyone works hard. Mr. Stamos cuts the meat. He cuts lamb, beef, and chicken into pieces. Mrs. Stamos cuts the vegetables. She cuts tomatoes, mushrooms, onions, and green peppers. She cooks rice and potatoes.

Nick and George serve the customers. They walk quickly with the food. They don't want it to get cold. It smells delicious!

C   Answer the questions.

1.   What kinds of food does the restaurant serve?

2.   Who works in the restaurant?

3.   What jobs do Nick's uncle and aunt do in the restaurant?

4.   Who is George?

5.   What job does George do?

6.   When does Nick serve food in the restaurant?

7.   When is the restaurant busy?

8.   What kinds of meat does Mr. Stamos cut into pieces?

9.   What vegetables does Mrs. Stamos cut?

10.   What does she cook?

11.   Why do Nikos and George walk quickly?

WHAT COLOUR ARE THE FOODS?

A   Match the words with the foods.

an apple

corn

carrots

an egg

bananas

an orange

lettuce

a tomato

butter

peas

grapes

rice

a pear

potatoes

a plum

B   Make a chart. Write the foods under the colours. Some foods can be more than one colour.

Red	Yellow	Orange	Green	Purple	White	Brown
grapes			grapes	grapes		

 **C**   Draw some other foods. Write the colours.

EATING OUT

LISTENING ACTIVITY 11

A   Look at the pictures of food. Match the words to the pictures.

1. a hamburger
2. a hot dog
3. fries (french fries)
4. a coke

5. a sandwich
6. a salad
7. coffee
8. pizza

B   Look at the pictures. Where are the people?

C   Read the questions with a partner.

D   Listen and answer the questions.

Kate's Order

1.   What kind of sandwich does Kate order?

2.   What else does she order?

3.   What does she order to drink?

4.   How much does it come to?

Michel's Order

1.   What does Michel order? (two things)

2.   What does he want on his hamburger?

3.   What does he order to drink?

4.   What does it come to?

Turn to page 91 for Exercise E.

Work in groups. Imagine you are in a restaurant. One person is the server. The other people are customers. Order some food from the menu below.

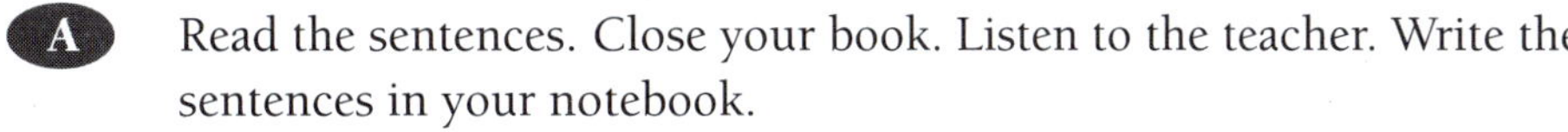

JOURNAL

A Read the sentences. Close your book. Listen to the teacher. Write the sentences in your notebook.

> I'm Mona. Lili and I eat lunch in a restaurant every Friday. We eat at Cafe Gina. The food is very good. I like the sandwiches. Lili likes the salads. We both like the coffee.

B Write about food you like to eat.

TEN-MINUTE GAMES AND ACTIVITIES

The Food Puzzle

Work with a partner. Write the words in the puzzle. Then find the hidden word.

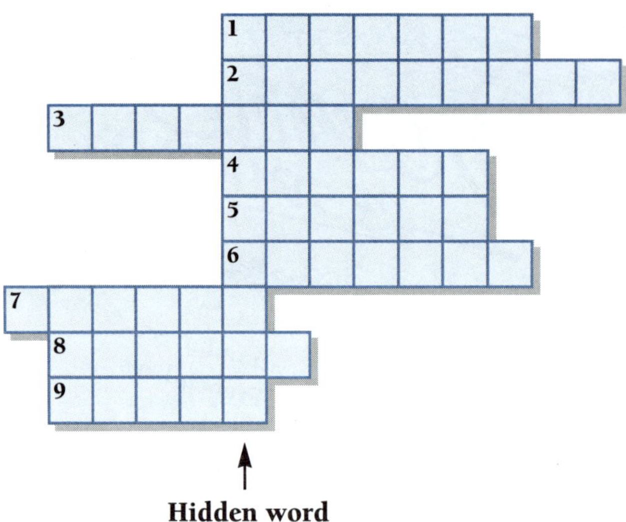

Hidden word

1. This is a very popular food for lunch or dinner. People cook it many different ways. They often eat it with potatoes or rice.

2. This is a popular food in a fast-food restaurant. It is meat that comes on a bun.

3. These vegetables are orange.

4. This food is made from milk. You can eat it in a sandwich.

5. This fruit has the same name as a colour.

6. This is a seafood. It is not a fish.

7. This long yellow fruit makes a good snack.

8. We use this vegetable to make french fries.

9. This popular fruit is red, yellow, or green.

Clue for the hidden word:

Everyone loves to eat _________________ for dessert or as a snack.

Quick Review

How many kinds of food do you remember? **Don't look back at the unit.**

Work in teams. The first team to have all the correct answers wins.

Find:

1. three vegetables that begin with **C**
2. three foods that are red
3. two cold drinks
4. two kinds of meat
5. three foods that are white
6. two vegetables that begin with **P**
7. two hot drinks that people like in the morning
8. three kinds of sandwiches
9. two things people eat for dessert
10. two foods that are orange
11. three foods that have four letters
12. three foods that are good in salads

Beginnings

Use the letters in the boxes to complete the words below. Some letters will not be used. They spell a word. Find the word.

gr	co	re	wh
or	bl	pu	lo
ur	ye	br	bl

__ __ d   __ __ o w n   __ __ a c k

__ __ a n g e   __ __ u e   __ __ e e n

__ __ l l o w   __ __ r p l e   __ __ i t e

Hidden word: __ __ __ __ __ __

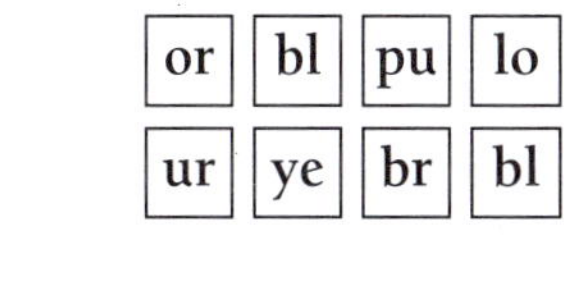

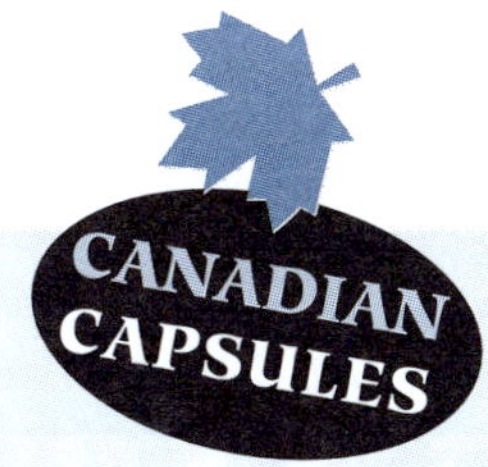

Bread is a basic food in Canada. Many Canadians eat bread two or three times a day. There are many different kinds of bread.

A SHOPPING LIST

LISTENING ACTIVITY 10

  **B**　Practise the conversations with a partner.

Ana and Carlos

Ana:　I'm going shopping for groceries. What do you want for supper?

Carlos:　I'd like fish for supper.

Ana:　OK. I'll get some fish. Do you want potatoes?

Carlos:　No, I don't want potatoes, but I'd like some rice.

Ana:　OK, I'll get some rice. Anything else?

Carlos:　Can you get some chocolate cookies for dessert?

Ana:　Sure, no problem. I think we need some coffee, too.

Carlos:　Yes, that's right. Don't forget the coffee.

Max and Olga

Max:　I'm going to the supermarket today. What do we need?

Olga:　We need milk and cheese, and some fruit. How about some oranges?

Max:　We don't need oranges. We have lots of oranges, but we need apples.

Olga:　OK, get some apples. Can you get some bananas too?

Max:　Sure. I'll get apples and bananas.

Jun and Tim

Jun:　I'm going shopping for groceries. What do we need?

Tim:　Can you get some lettuce? I want to make a salad for lunch.

Jun:　Just lettuce? How about tomatoes and celery?

Tim:　I don't like tomatoes, but we can get celery and cucumber.

Jun:　OK, I'll get lettuce, celery, and cucumber.

EATING OUT

LISTENING ACTIVITY 11

E   Listen and write the words. Use the worksheet.

Kate's Order

Server: Can I help you?

Kate: Yes, I'd _______________ a sandwich please.

Server: What kind?

Kate: I'd like _______________ cheese sandwich, please.

Server: OK, a cheese sandwich. Anything _______________?

Kate: Yes, a salad.

Server: Anything _______________ drink?

Kate: Yes, coffee please.

Server: That comes to $5.15.

Michel's Order

Server: _______________ I help you?

Michel: Yes, _______________ like a hamburger and fries, please.

Server: _______________ you want mustard and relish _______________ the hamburger?

Michel: Just mustard, please.

Server: Anything _______________ drink?

Michel: Yes, _______________ large coke please.

Server: That _______________ to $4.70.

F   Practise the conversations with a partner.

UNIT 7

THE BODY AND HEALTH

HOW DO YOU FEEL?

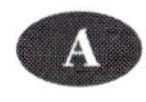

A Work with a partner. Match the pictures with the words.

1. hungry
2. thirsty
3. tired
4. hot
5. cold
6. happy
7. angry
8. nervous

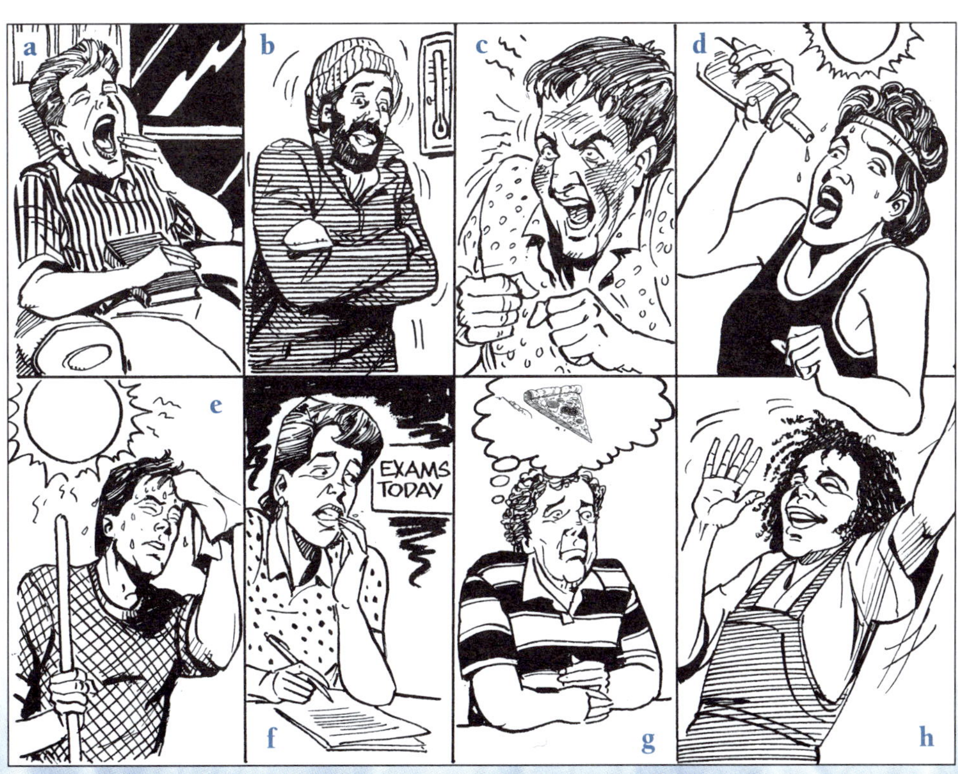

B   What can you do? Match the questions with the answers.

1. You are hungry.	a) You can close the window.
2. You are thirsty.	b) You can relax.
3. You are tired.	c) You can sleep.
4. You are hot.	d) You can drink.
5. You are cold.	e) You can open the window.
6. You are nervous.	f) You can eat.

THE BODY

A   Practise with the teacher. Look at the pictures. Listen and repeat.

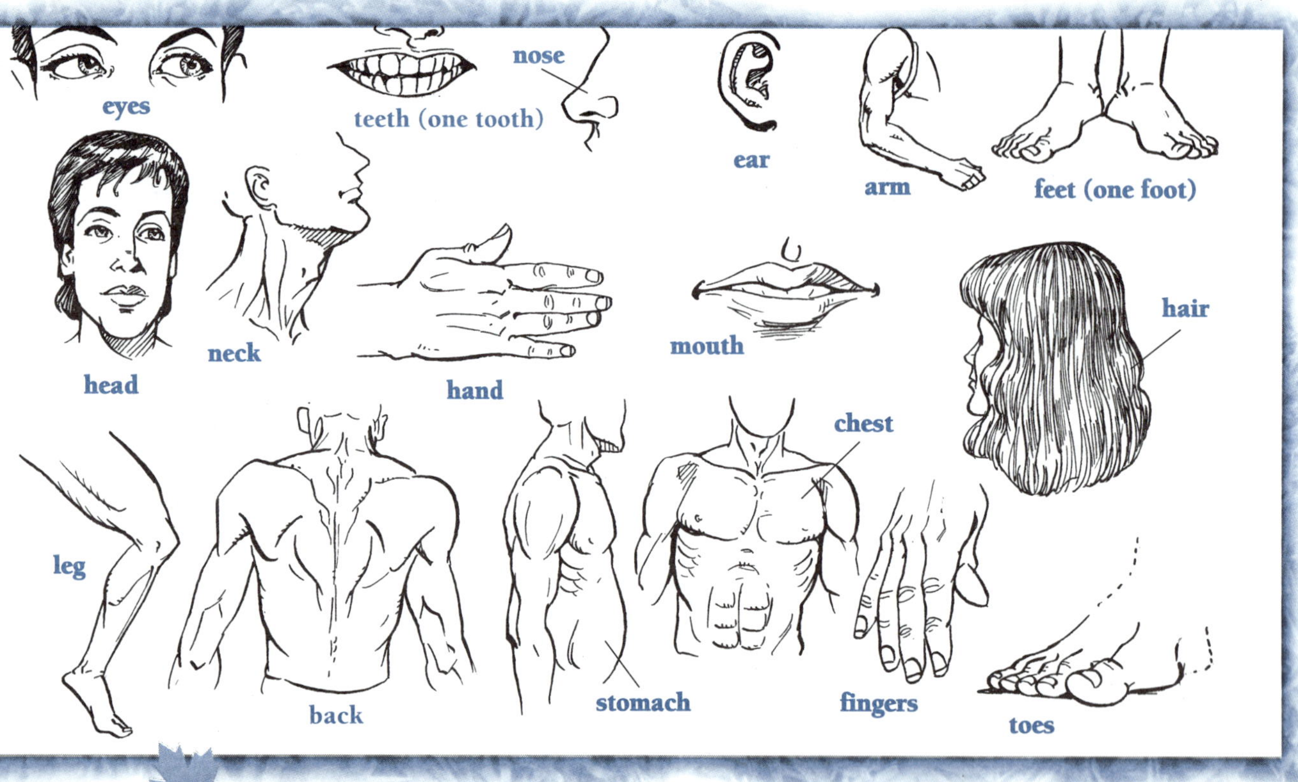

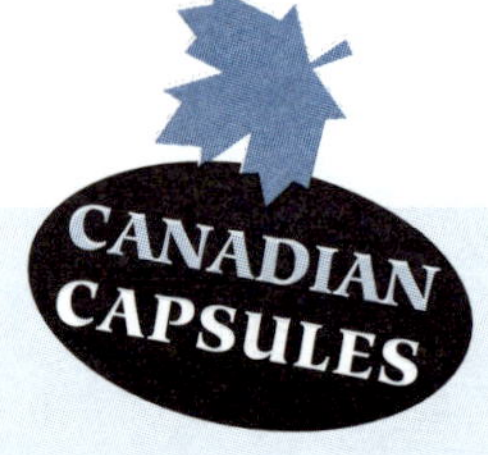

In Canada, most people have a "family doctor." This doctor knows their medical history. When they have a medical problem, they call their family doctor.

B   Look at the picture. Write the name for each part of the body.

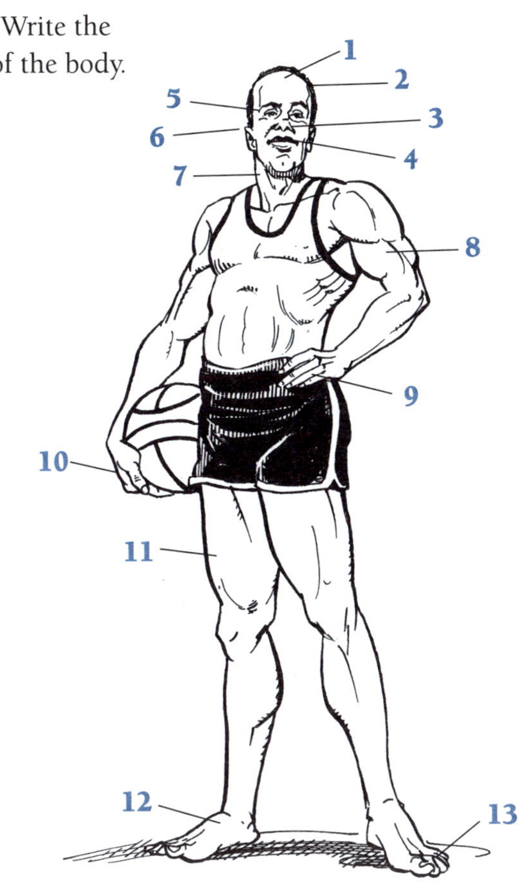

GRAMMAR FOCUS   Present Simple Tense: Questions

Question	
do I	
do you	
does he	
does she	work?
does it	
do we	
do you	
do they	

 **STOP**   Use **do** or **does** before the subject.

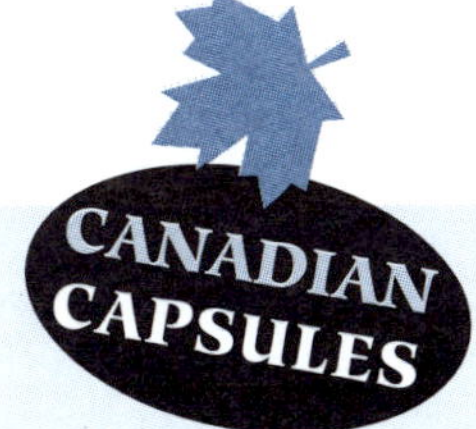
CANADIAN CAPSULES

If you have a serious medical problem—for example, if you have an accident—go to the emergency room of a hospital right away. If you have a cold, or a sore back, do not go to the emergency room. Go to your family doctor or to a clinic in your neighbourhood.

A   Change these sentences to questions.

1.   Mona brushes her hair every morning.
2.   Ana and Carlos cook eggs for breakfast.
3.   Jun shops for food every Saturday.
4.   Lili works in a bank.
5.   Max drives a taxi.
6.   Kate buys vegetables at the market.
7.   Olga and Max eat chicken on Fridays.
8.   Masha plays games with her friends.
9.   Michel walks to work.
10.   Carlos reads the newspaper every morning.

B   Make questions.

> wakes up late/Mike   **Does Mike wake up late?**

1.   brushes her hair/Mona
2.   feels tired/she
3.   eat in the cafeteria/the students
4.   cuts her hair every month/Sylvia
5.   takes a shower every morning/Andrea
6.   begins at two o'clock/English class
7.   brush our teeth after lunch/we
8.   has a moustache/Stephan
9.   buy vitamins/Paula and Gaby
10.   washes his hair every day/Mario

C   Some verbs are wrong. Find the errors and correct them.

> Does Patrick wears glasses? ✘   Does Patrick **wear** glasses? ✔

1.   Do Manuel and Sandra walk to school?
2.   Do Pierre take vitamins?
3.   Does he have a moustache?
4.   Does Lee knows Cindy?
5.   Does Suzanna and Ricardo shop at the market?
6.   Do they get up early?
7.   Do we need sunglasses today?
8.   Do you has a cold?
9.   Do your brother cut his hair often?
10.   Does he have brown eyes?

SICK

A Match the words to the pictures.

1. a headache
2. an earache
3. a cold
4. a fever

B Practise with the teacher. Look at the pictures. Talk about what you see.

C   Read the story.

Sick

Masha doesn't feel well today. She is very tired. She has an earache. She also has a cold. Olga takes her to the doctor. The doctor examines Masha. First she looks in her ears. Then she takes Masha's temperature. Masha has a fever. The doctor tells Masha to rest in bed. She tells her to drink water and juice. Soon she will be well.

D   Answer the questions with a partner.

1.   How does Masha feel?

2.   What does Masha have? (Name two problems.)

3.   Where do Masha and Olga go?

4.   What does the doctor do? (two things)

5.   What does the doctor tell Masha to do? (two things)

AT THE DOCTOR

LISTENING ACTIVITY 12

A   Practise with the teacher. Look at the pictures. Listen and repeat.

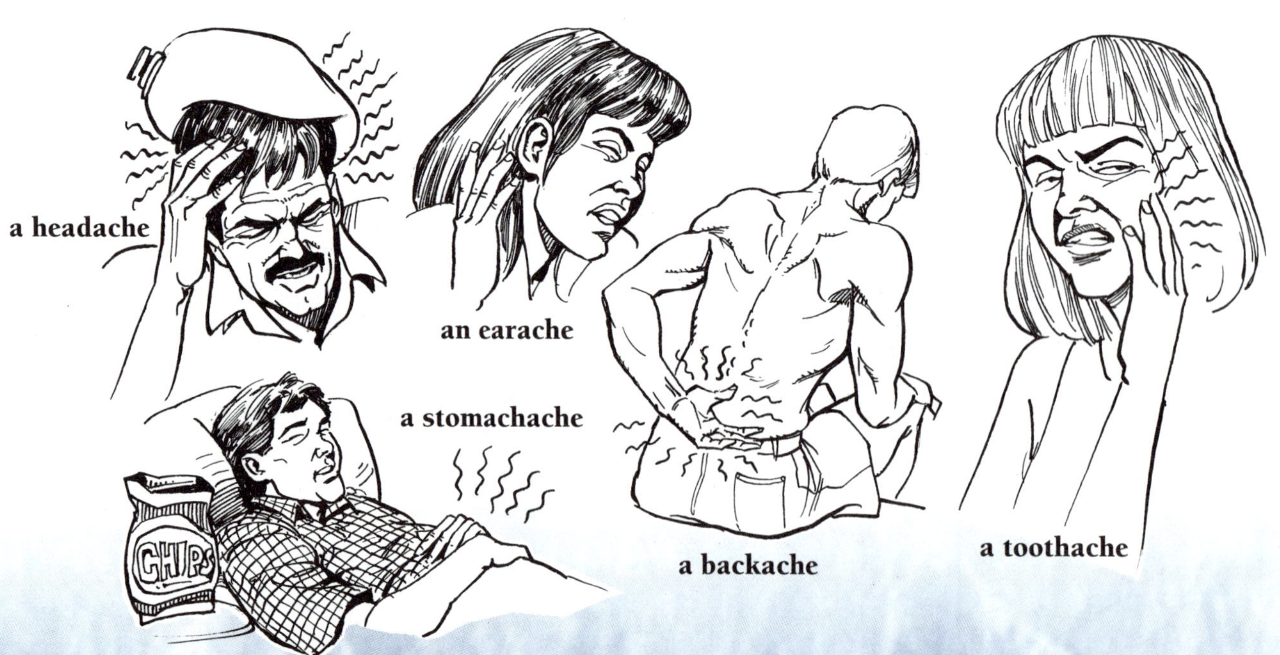

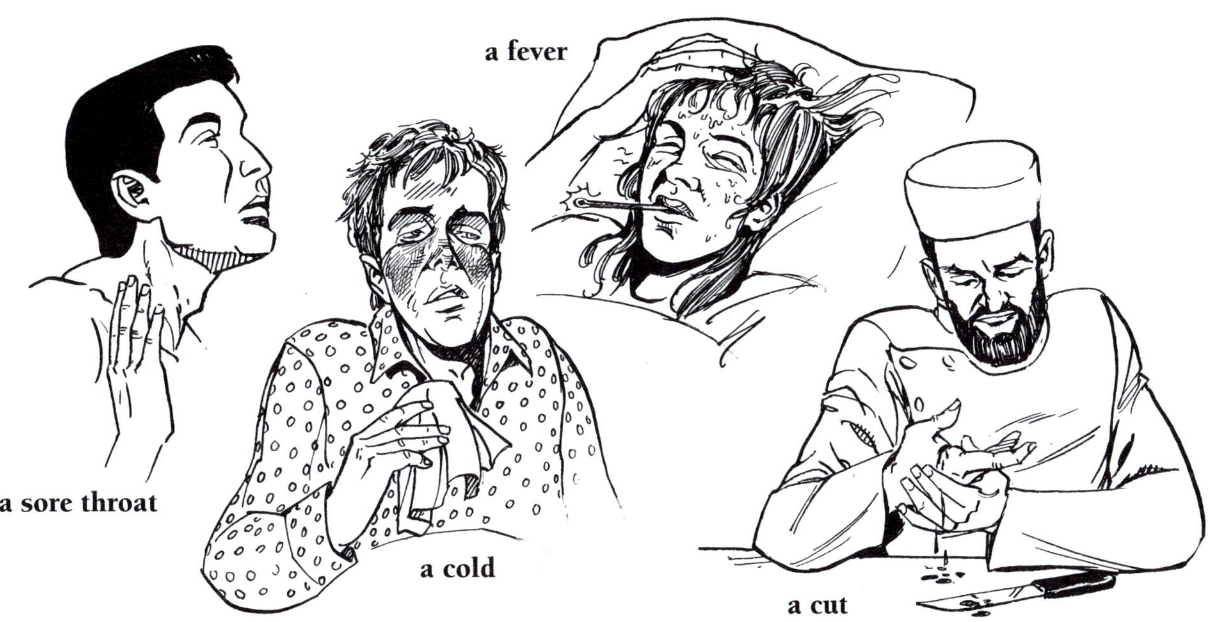

B Complete the sentences.

ear fever stomachache backache sick toothache rest head

1. My stomach hurts. I have a ________________.

2. I can't go to work. I'm ________________ today.

3. I have an earache. My ________________ hurts.

4. I have a cold. I need to ________________ today.

5. I have a headache. My ________________ hurts.

6. I feel hot. I have a ________________.

7. My back hurts. I have a ________________.

8. I have a ________________. I have to go to the dentist.

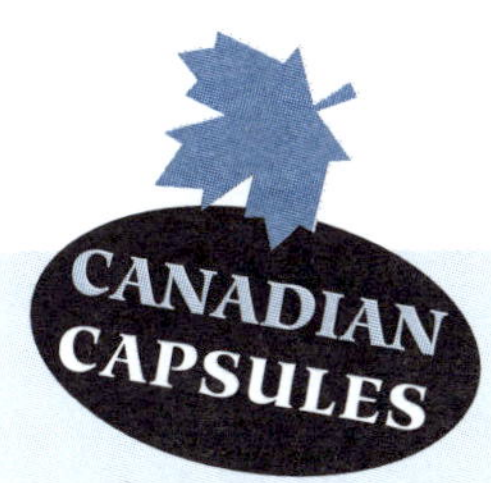

CANADIAN CAPSULES

Many people get colds and flu in the winter months or at the change of seasons. Most people get better without any medical help, but if you don't get better after a few days, see your doctor.

C   Listen and answer the questions. Write "yes" or "no."

Jun

1. Jun has a stomachache.
2. Jun has a fever.
3. Jun feels tired.
4. The doctor will examine Jun.

Masha

1. Masha has an earache.
2. Masha has a cold.
3. Masha has a fever.

Turn to page 106 for Exercise D.

TALK ABOUT IT

Work with a partner. Write a new conversation about going to the doctor.
Act it out.

AT THE DRUGSTORE

A   Match the words to the pictures.

**soap   band aids   shampoo   a toothbrush   tissues
toothpaste   aspirin   a comb   a brush   ointment**

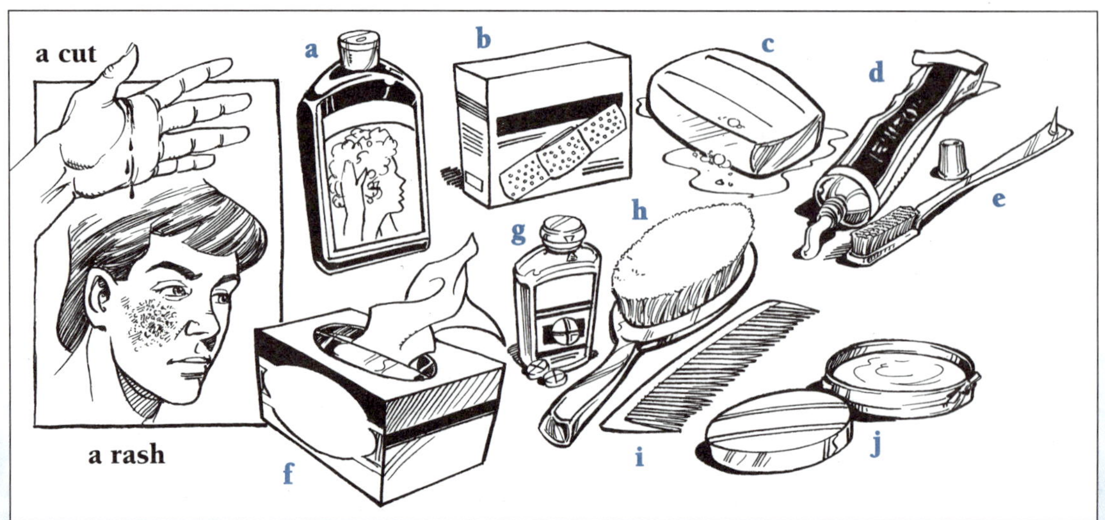

B   Match:

1. to wash your hair	a) band aids
2. to brush your teeth	b) ointment
3. to comb your hair	c) a toothbrush and toothpaste
4. for a cold	d) shampoo
5. for a headache	e) a comb and brush
6. to wash	f) tissues
7. for a cut	g) soap
8. for a rash	h) aspirin

TAKING MEDICINE

A   Practise with the teacher. Look at the pictures. Listen and repeat.

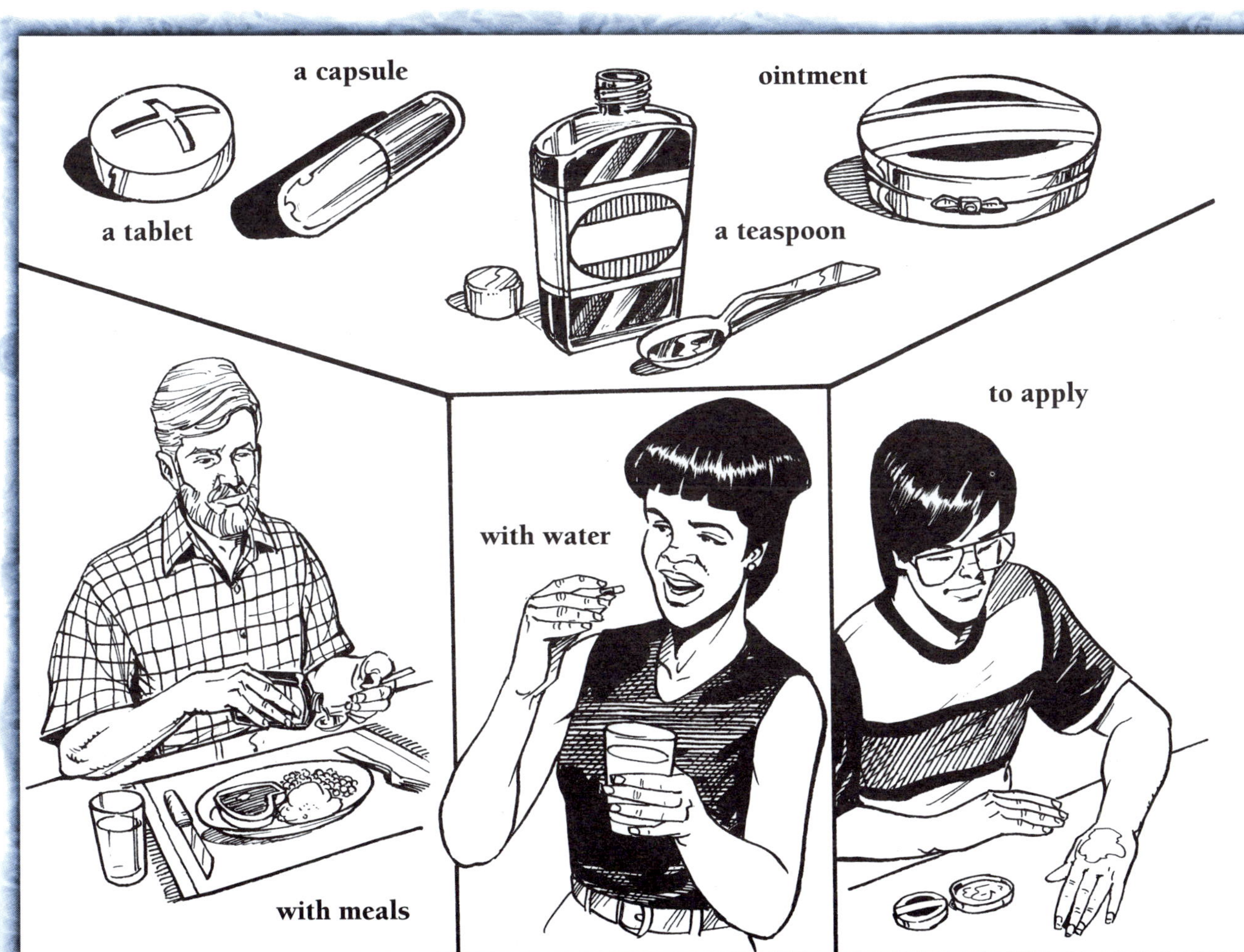

B   Match the pictures to the sentences below.

1.   Take two capsules twice a day, with water.

2.   Take two teaspoons three times a day.

3.   Take one teaspoon three times a day with meals.

4.   Use the ointment twice a day.

5.   Take two tablets three times a day.

6.   Take one tablet twice a day, morning and evening.

HOW DO I TAKE IT?

LISTENING ACTIVITY 13

  **A** Read the questions with a partner.

  **B** Listen to the conversations and choose the correct answers.

Ana

1. Ana needs to take:

    a) one capsule three times a day

    b) three capsules once a day

    c) two capsules three times a day

2. Ana needs to take the capsules:

    a) before meals

    b) with meals

    c) after meals

Mona

1. Mona needs to take:

    a) two teaspoons twice a day

    b) one teaspoon twice a day

    c) two teaspoons once a day

2. Mona takes the medicine:

    a) with lunch and dinner

    b) in the morning and in the evening

    c) with breakfast

3. She takes the medicine:

    a) with food

    b) on its own

    c) with water

Turn to page 107 for Exercise C.

TALK ABOUT IT

Work in a group. Imagine you have to take medicine. Talk about the questions you need to ask the doctor or the pharmacist.

A Read the sentences. Close your book. Listen to the teacher. Write the sentences in your notebook.

I'm Jun. I am sick today. I have a headache and a stomachache. I am very tired.

B How do you feel today? Write about how you feel.

TEN-MINUTE GAMES AND ACTIVITIES

Opposites

Match the opposites from Box A and Box B.

Box A

fingers
chest
patient
good
arms
well
wake up   hot
hungry
open
sad   morning
eat
hands
nervous
right

Box A

happy
full
feet
cold   left
back   drink
sick   bad
go to sleep
relaxed
close
legs
evening   toes
doctor

Your Health

Work in pairs to complete the crossword puzzle.

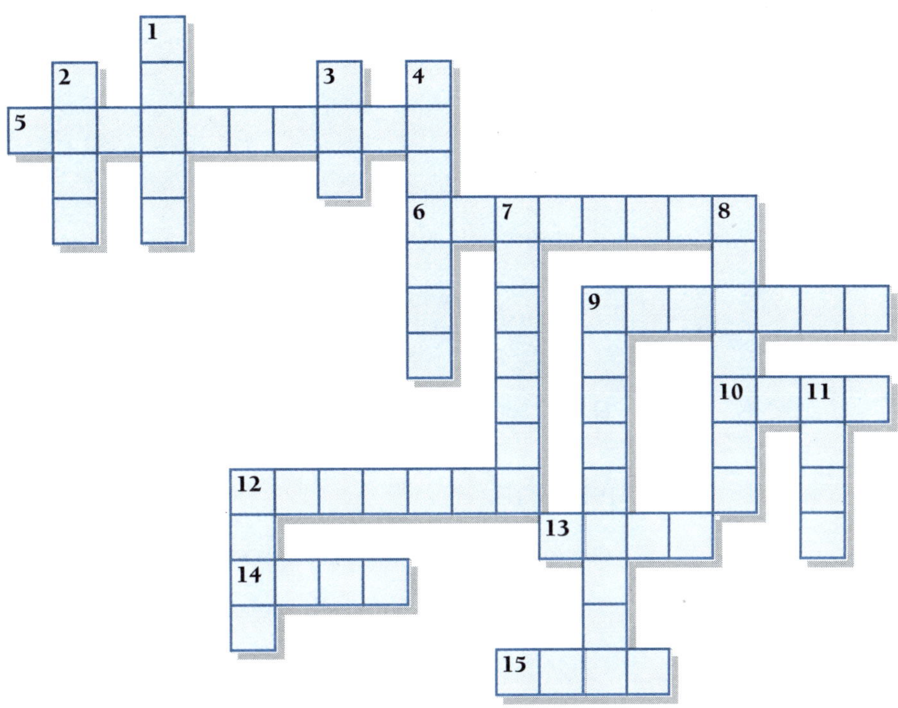

Across

5. You brush your teeth with toothpaste and a _________________.

6. When you are sick, you sometimes have to take _________________.

9. When you are _________________, you drink.

10. It is common to catch a _________________ in winter.

12. We have five _________________ on each hand.

13. We listen and hear with our _________________.

14. We see with our _________________.

15. We have five _________________ on each foot.

Down

1. You need to drink _________________ when you take medicine.

2. We wash with _________________ and water.

3. You need a band aid if you have a _________________.

4. We use _________________ to wash our hair.

7. _________________ are people who help us when we are sick.

8. If your ear hurts, you have an _________________.

9. You should go to the dentist if you have a _________________.

11. You use your _________________ to walk.

12. Our toes are on our _________________.

AT THE DOCTOR

LISTENING ACTIVITY 12

  **D** Practise the conversations with a partner.

Jun

Doctor: Hello, Jun. What's wrong?

Jun: I don't feel well, doctor. I have a stomachache.

Doctor: Do you have a fever?

Jun: No, just a stomachache. I feel very tired.

Doctor: OK, Jun. We'll examine you to see what's wrong.

Masha

Doctor: Hi, Masha. What's wrong?

Masha: I don't feel well. My ear hurts.

Doctor: Olga, does she have a cold?

Olga: Yes she does.

Doctor: Does she have a fever?

Olga: Yes, a little.

Doctor: OK, Masha. We'll examine you to see what's wrong.

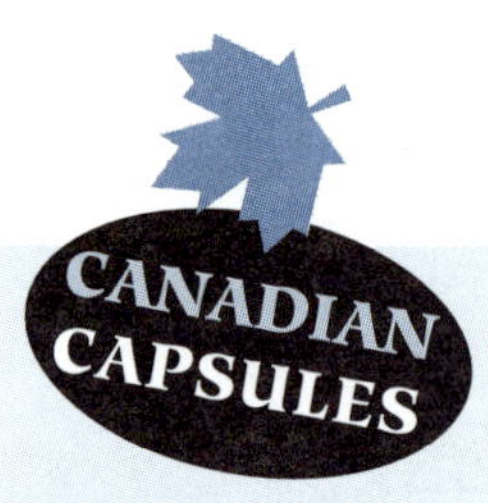

CANADIAN CAPSULES If you already take medicine, be sure to tell the pharmacist before you get a new one. Some medicines can make you very sick if you take them together.

HOW DO I TAKE IT?

LISTENING ACTIVITY 13

 **C**   Listen and write the words. Use the worksheet.

Ana

Pharmacist: Here's your medicine. Take one capsule _______________ times a day.

Ana: Do I take _______________ with my meals?

Pharmacist: Yes. Take the capsules with _______________ breakfast, lunch, and dinner.

Ana: OK. I take one capsule three times _______________ day, with breakfast, lunch, and dinner.

Pharmacist: That_______________ correct.

Mona

Pharmacist: Here_______________ your medicine. Take one teaspoon _______________ a day.

Mona: I understand. I take one teaspoon twice a day.

Pharmacist: Yes, take _______________ in the morning and in _______________ evening.

Mona: Do I take it with _______________ meals?

Pharmacist: No, take it with water, when you wake _______________, and before you go _______________ sleep.

 **D**   Practise the conversations with a partner.

A Look at the picture. Find these things:

1. a house
2. an apartment building
3. an elevator
4. a tree
5. grass
6. flowers

B   Read the story with a partner.

Houses and Apartments

Michel lives in an apartment building. There are trees in front of the building. There are fourteen floors in the building. Michel lives on the ninth floor. He takes the elevator to his apartment.

Jun lives in a small apartment building. The building has three floors. Jun lives on the second floor. He walks up the stairs to his apartment.

Lili lives with her aunt and uncle. Their house has eight rooms. The rooms are on one floor. The house has a big window. She can see trees, flowers, and grass in front of the house.

Kate lives in an apartment. There are twenty floors in the building. Kate lives on the fifteenth floor. She takes the elevator to her apartment. She can see the city from her living-room window.

C   Write the name or names of the people.

1. Who has trees in front of the building?

2. Who has eight rooms in their house?

3. Who lives on the fifteenth floor?

4. Who walks up the stairs?

5. Who takes the elevator?

6. Who has a big window?

7. Who can see the city?

8. Who has one floor in their house?

9. Who lives on the second floor?

10. Who lives on the ninth floor?

CANADIAN CAPSULES

Most houses or apartments in Canada have one or more bedrooms, a living room, a kitchen, and a bathroom. Bigger homes have more bedrooms or bathrooms, and extra rooms, such as a dining room or a den.

ROOMS IN THE HOUSE

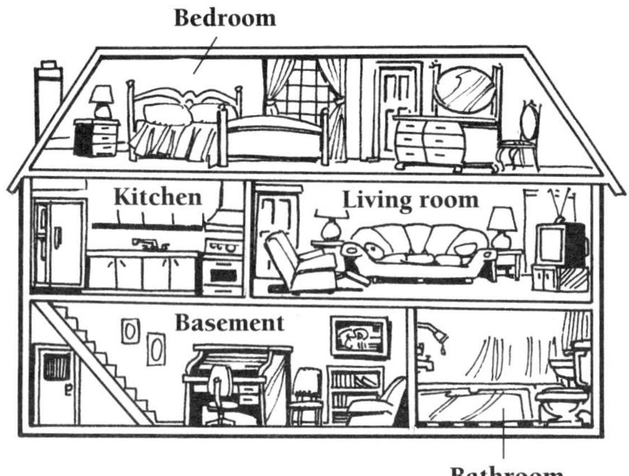

Apartment A

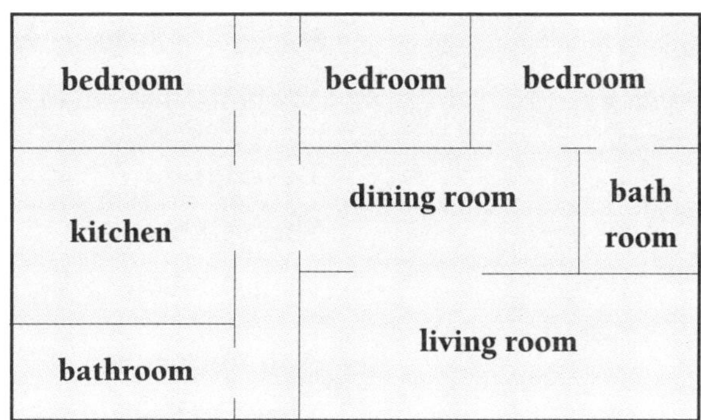

Apartment B

Apartment C

A Work with a partner. Look at the pictures. Copy and complete the chart.

		Apartment A	Apartment B	Apartment C
1.	four rooms		✗	
2.	three bedrooms			
3.	eight rooms			
4.	one bathroom			
5.	a living room			
6.	a dining room			
7.	two bedrooms			
8.	one bedroom			
9.	a kitchen			
10.	two bathrooms			

GRAMMAR FOCUS — Verb "Have"

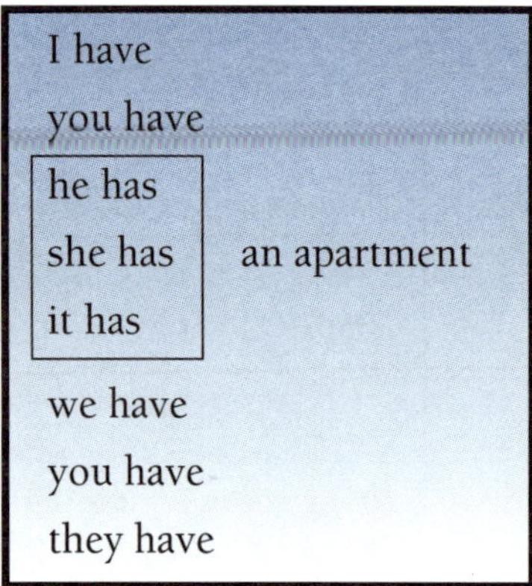

Use the verb **have** with:

Possession

We have a dog.

My house has small windows.

Description

She has short hair.

He has a moustache.

Appointments

I have a class at five.

He has a doctor's appointment on Friday.

The Weather

Canada has cold winters.

Singapore has hot weather.

Sickness

She has a headache.

He has a cold.

A   Use the correct form of **have**.

1. We _________ an appointment at the dentist.

2. My parents _________ a new car.

3. Sam _________ an apartment in my building.

4. I _________ a cold.

5. My friend _________ a moustache.

6. She _________ long hair.

7. Vancouver _________ rainy weather.

8.   Pat and Jim __________ a dog and a cat.

9.   Those people __________ a garden.

10.   They __________ a tree near their house.

B   Some sentences are wrong. Find the errors in the verbs and correct them.

1.   Michel has a big apartment.

2.   Roberto and Carla have two children.

3.   Stephan has a new house.

4.   You has a brother.

5.   Toronto has cold winters.

6.   He have a car and a bicycle.

7.   We has a cat.

8.   The house has five rooms.

9.   You has a new couch.

10.   She have a large kitchen.

AN APARTMENT FOR RENT

LISTENING ACTIVITY 14

    **A**   Read the questions with a partner.

    **B**   Listen and answer the questions.

First Apartment

1.   How many rooms does the apartment have?

2.   How much is the rent?

3.   What is wrong with the apartment? (two things)

Second Apartment

1.   How many apartments are for rent?

2.   How much is the rent for the smaller apartment?

3.   When can Michel see the apartment?

4.   What is the address?

Turn to page 123 for Exercise C.

TALK ABOUT IT

Work in a group. Imagine you want to rent an apartment. Talk about what kind of apartment you want. How many rooms do you need? How much rent would you pay?

THINGS IN THE HOUSE

A Look at the pictures. Match the words to the pictures.

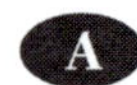

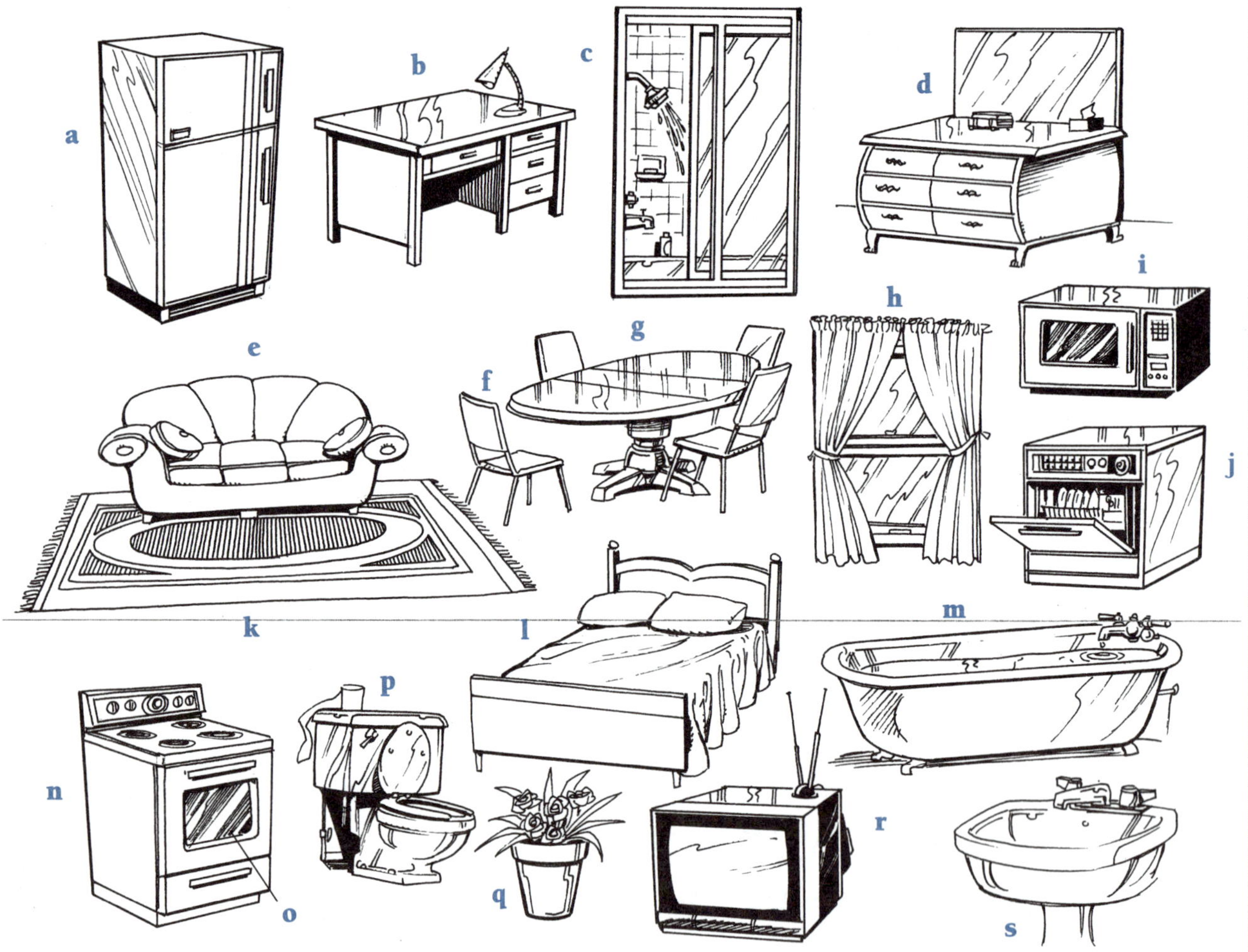

bed table couch/sofa bathtub refrigerator television (TV) stove oven chairs dishwasher desk sink bureau/dresser rug toilet shower curtains microwave plant

B   Work with a partner. Make a chart. Put the things in the rooms. Some things can go in more than one room.

Kitchen	Bedroom	Living room	Bathroom

MY PLACE

Draw a picture of your house or apartment. Label the rooms. Draw the furniture.

TALK ABOUT IT

Work in a group. Show the pictures of your house or apartment. Talk about where you live.

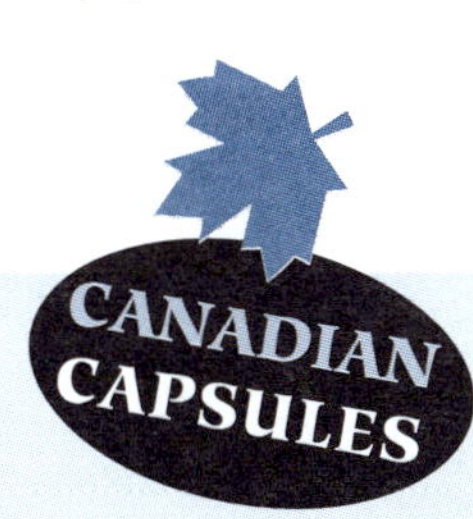

CANADIAN CAPSULES

Winters are cold in most parts of Canada, but Canadians know how to keep warm. Homes are well heated, and windows and doors are made to keep the heat inside.

A FURNISHED APARTMENT

Jun and his friend Tim share an apartment. The apartment is furnished. When they move in, the owner gives them a list of things in the kitchen.

 Read the list. Look at the picture on page 117. Write what is missing.

> **Things missing**
> In the cupboard: 2 plates
> In the first drawer: 1 spoon

In the cupboard:

6 plates

6 bowls

8 glasses

6 cups

In the first drawer:

6 spoons

6 forks

6 knives

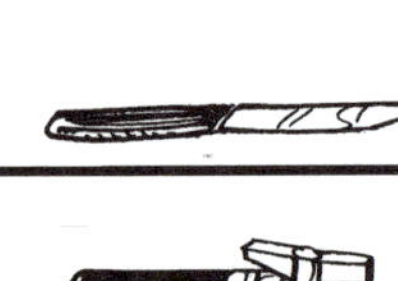 1 can opener

In the second drawer:

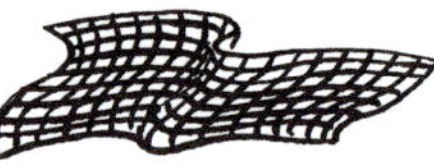 3 dish towels

On the shelf:

 2 pots with lids

 1 frying pan

On the counter:

a coffee maker

a toaster

 a tea kettle

cupboard
freezer
shelf
stove
refrigerator
(fridge)
dish drainer
taps
sink
oven
dishwashing
soap
first drawer
second drawer

Question Words "What," "Where," "Who"

Where   asks about location.

Who   asks about a person or people.

What   asks about things.

A   Match the questions to the answers.

1.	Where is your apartment?	a)	on the counter
2.	Who are your friends?	b)	my sister
3.	What is in the refrigerator?	c)	Olga and Max
4.	Where is the toaster	d)	spoons and forks
5.	What is in the drawer?	e)	on the ninth floor
6.	Who is this girl?	f)	a chicken

B   Copy the chart. Put the words in the correct place.

Where	Who	What
in the elevator	Olga and Max	a spoon

1.	Olga and Max	11.	the couch
2.	in the elevator	12.	in the kitchen
3.	in the cupboard	13.	the owner
4.	a spoon	14.	the pot
5.	on the ninth floor	15.	on the counter
6.	in the drawer	16.	Ana and Carlos
7.	Michel	17.	the can opener
8.	in the refrigerator	18.	the children
9.	in the sink	19.	a dish towel
10.	the dishwasher	20.	my neighbours

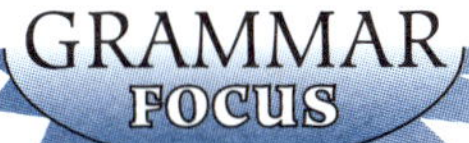

GRAMMAR FOCUS

Prepositions of Place

in **on** **under** **between** **beside**

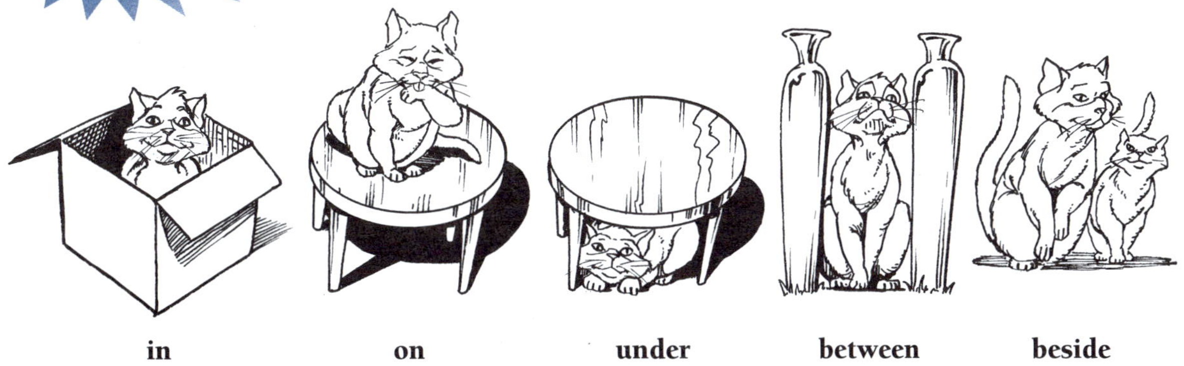

A Look at the picture below. Complete the paragraph.

Masha was in the kitchen. Now it's a big mess. The cereal is ______________ the counter. The milk is not ______________ the fridge. It is ______________ the toaster. A spoon is ______________ the table. A dish is ______________ a dish towel. A glass is ______________ the coffee maker and the kettle.

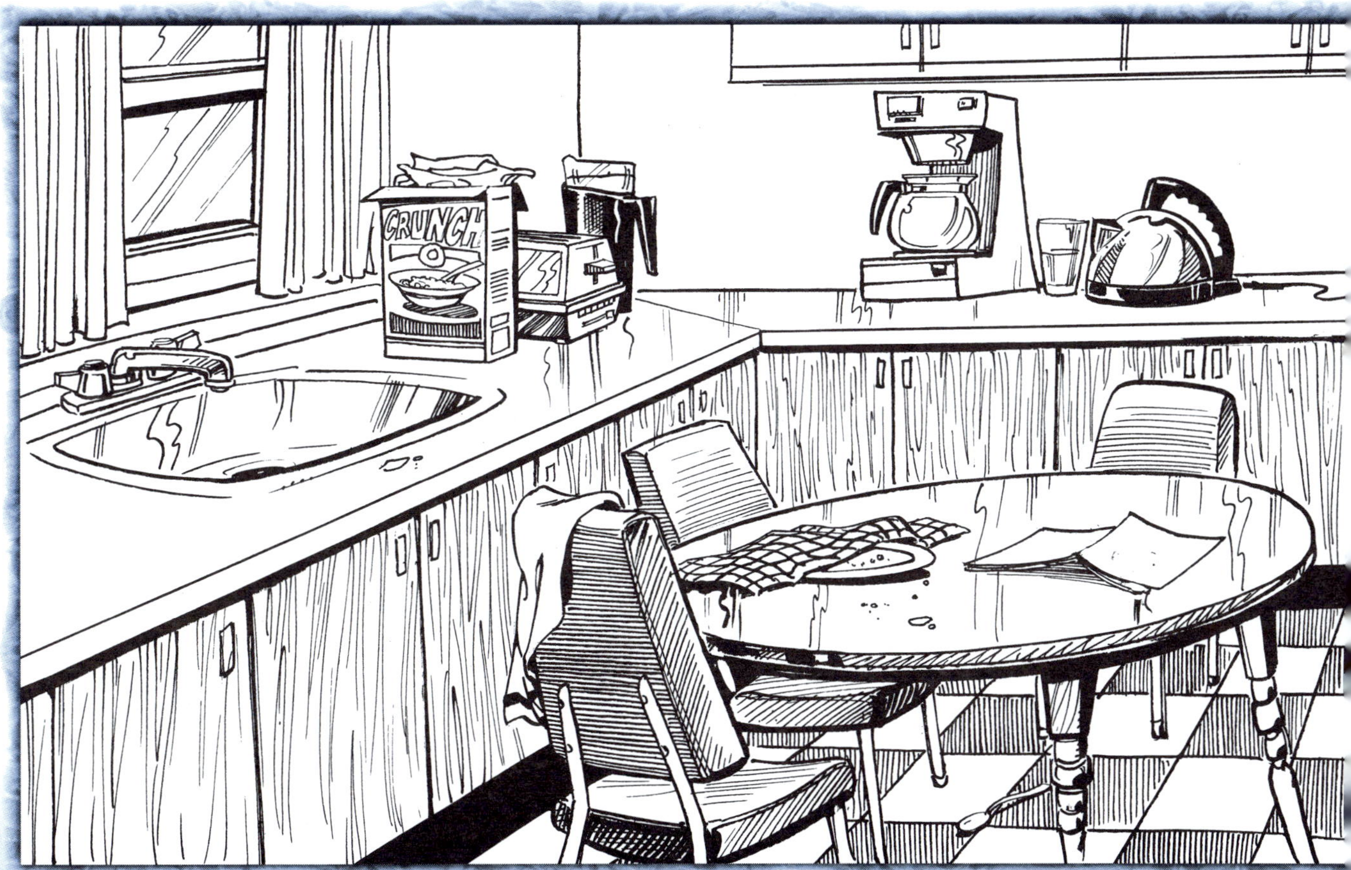

I HAVE A PROBLEM

LISTENING ACTIVITY 15

A   Match the pictures to the problems.

1. The oven doesn't work.
2. The refrigerator is broken.
3. The doorbell doesn't work.
4. The tap leaks.
5. The sink is blocked.
6. There's no heat.

B   Read the questions with a partner.

C   Listen to the conversations. Choose the correct answers.

Olga

1. Olga is in apartment:
    a) 397
    b) 307

2. Olga's problem is:
    a) her sink is blocked
    b) the tap leaks

Michel

1. Michel is in apartment:
    a) 912
    b) 921

2. Michel's apartment is:
    a) too hot
    b) too cold

3. The manager says:
    a) There is a problem in the building.
    b) It's very cold outside.

Jun

1. The manager will be back at:
    a) 10:00
    b) 11:00

2. Jun is in apartment:
    a) 2E
    b) 2B

3. Jun's problem is:
    a) The stove doesn't work.
    b) The fridge doesn't work.

Turn to page 124 for Exercise D.

TALK ABOUT IT

Choose one of these problems in your home or apartment:

1. The tap drips.
2. It's too hot.
3. The refrigerator doesn't work.
4. The ceiling is leaking.
5. The toilet is blocked.

Work with a partner. Write a conversation about calling the manager. Act it out.

JOURNAL

 **A**   Read the sentences. Close your book. Listen to the teacher. Write the sentences in your notebook.

> Olga and Max have a new apartment. The apartment is on the fifth floor. The apartment has two bedrooms. It has a big kitchen and living room. Olga and Max are very happy.

 **B**   Write about your house or apartment.

Categories

Put these words into categories. There are six groups, with three words in each group.

bedroom	fork	plate
chair	garden	refrigerator
couch	glass	spoon
cup	kitchen	stove
dishwasher	knife	table
flowers	living room	tree

Find Someone

Walk around the room and ask questions to find people who have the things on the list. When a student answers "yes," write his or her name. The first person to finish is the winner.

Ask: Do you have…?

Answer: Yes, I do. No, I don't.

Find someone who has:

1. a large apartment
2. a small apartment
3. an apartment with two bedrooms
4. a dog
5. an elevator in his or her building
6. a tree near their window
7. a cat
8. a dishwasher
9. a microwave oven
10. a coffee maker
11. noisy neighbours
12. a garden

Beginnings

Use the letters in the boxes to complete the words below. Some letters will not be used. They spell a word. Find the word.

gl	re	si	ap	ba
ar	sp	tm	di	co
sh	kn	dr	wi	ch
ta	en	st	to	ts

__ __ f r i g e r a t o r   __ __ s h w a s h e r   __ __ n k

__ __ o w e r   __ __ a i r   __ __ b l e

__ __ t h   __ __ i f e   __ __ o v e

__ __ o o n   __ __ n d o w   __ __ a s s

__ __ a s t e r   __ __ u c h   __ __ a w e r

Hidden word: __ __ __ __ __ __ __ __ __ __ __

AN APARTMENT FOR RENT

LISTENING ACTIVITY 14

 **C**   Listen and write the words. Use the worksheet.

First Apartment

Michel: Hello. Do you ____________ an apartment for rent?

Owner: Yes, I ____________.

Michel: How many rooms ____________ it have?

Owner: It ____________ five rooms.

Michel: And how much ____________ the rent?

Owner: It's $725 per month.

Michel: Oh, that's ____________ expensive. And it's too big. I live alone. Thanks anyway.

Owner: You're welcome.

Second Apartment

Michel: ____________ you have an apartment ____________ rent?

Owner: Yes, I have ____________ apartments ____________ rent. One has ____________ rooms, and the other has three rooms.

Michel: How ____________ is the apartment with three rooms?

Owner: It's $400 per month.

Michel: That sounds good. ____________ I see it tomorrow?

Owner: Sure. You ____________ see it tomorrow afternoon. The address is ____________ Clark Street.

Michel: OK, that's ____________ Clark Street. Thank you.

  **D**   Practise the conversations with a partner.

I HAVE A PROBLEM

LISTENING ACTIVITY 15

  **D**   Practise the conversations with a partner.

Olga

Olga: Can I speak to the manager, please?

Manager: Speaking. Can I help you?

Olga: Yes, this is Olga Kuslov, in apartment 307.

Manager: What's the problem?

Olga: My kitchen sink is blocked. There's water everywhere.

Manager: I'll be up right away.

Olga: Thank you.

Michel

Michel: Can I speak to the manager, please?

Manager: Speaking. Can I help you?

Michel: This is Michel Banon, in apartment 912.

Manager: What's the problem?

Michel: I have no heat. It's freezing here.

Manager: Yes, I know. There's a problem in the building. I'll call you back.

Michel: Thank you.

Jun

Jun:	Can I speak to the manager, please?
Woman:	He isn't here right now. He'll be back at 11:00. Can I take a message?
Jun:	Yes, this is Jun Kim in apartment 2B. I have a problem.
Woman:	What is the problem?
Jun:	My stove doesn't work. Can he come soon? I want to cook dinner.
Woman:	I'll give him the message.
Jun:	Thank you.

 **A** Look and practise with the teacher.

**1 cent
OR a penny**

**5 cents
OR a nickel**

**10 cents
OR a dime**

**25 cents
OR a quarter**

**1 dollar
OR a loonie**

a five-dollar bill

a twenty-dollar bill

2 dollars

a ten-dollar bill

a fifty-dollar bill

B   Match the amounts to the coins and bills.

a) 1¢   e) $1   i) $20

b) 5¢   f) $2   j) $50

c) 10¢   g) $5

d) 25¢   h) $10

1

2

3

4

5

6

7

8

9

10

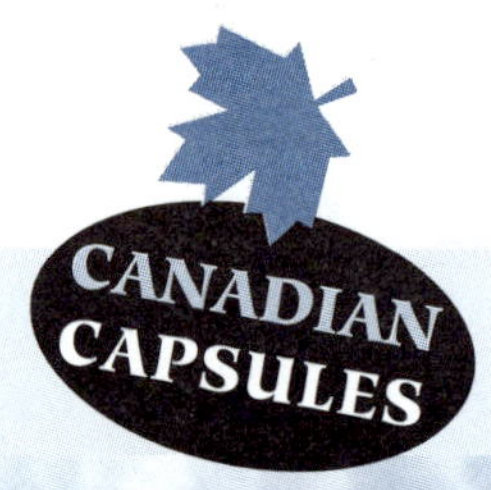

CANADIAN CAPSULES

Canadians have to pay their income tax by April 30 every year.

C   Match the amounts to the coins and bills.

a) $6

b)   3¢

c)   35¢

d)   20¢

e) $1

f)   14¢

g) $4

h)   75¢

i)   30¢

j)   21¢

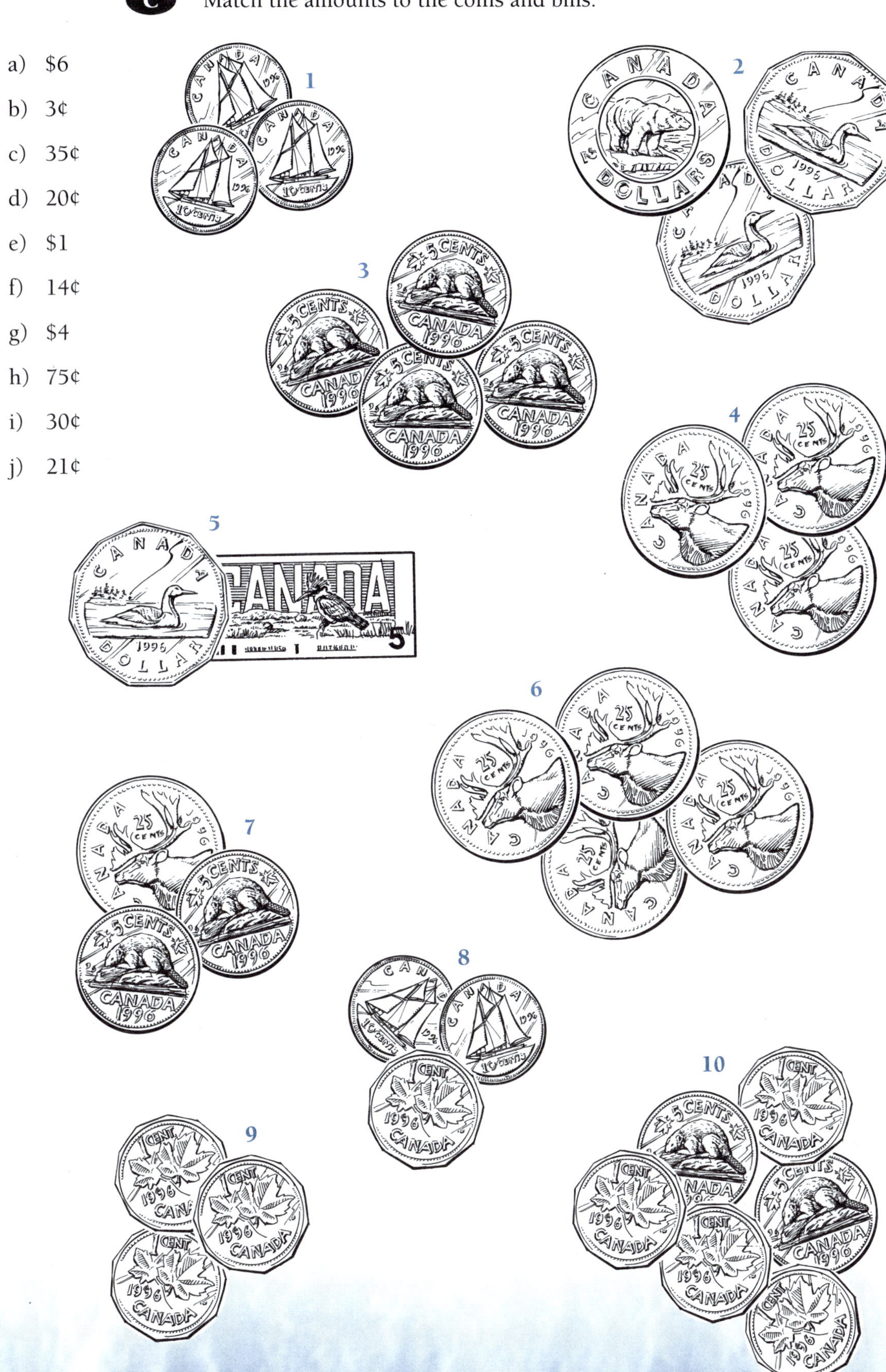

D Listen to the teacher. Write the amounts you hear. Use your notebook.

$3.25

COUNTING MONEY

Write the amounts.

LISTENING ACTIVITY **16**

Olga and Max are in a store. Listen to the conversations.

 **A** Read the questions with a partner.

 **B** Listen and answer the questions.

Olga

1. What does Olga like?

2. How much is the first one?

3. How much is the second one?

4. How much does it come to, with tax?

Max

1. What does Max like?

2. How much is it?

3. How much is the second one?

4. What does it come to, with tax?

Turn to page 144 for Exercise C.

CLOTHES

Look at the pictures. Work with a partner to name and label the clothes.

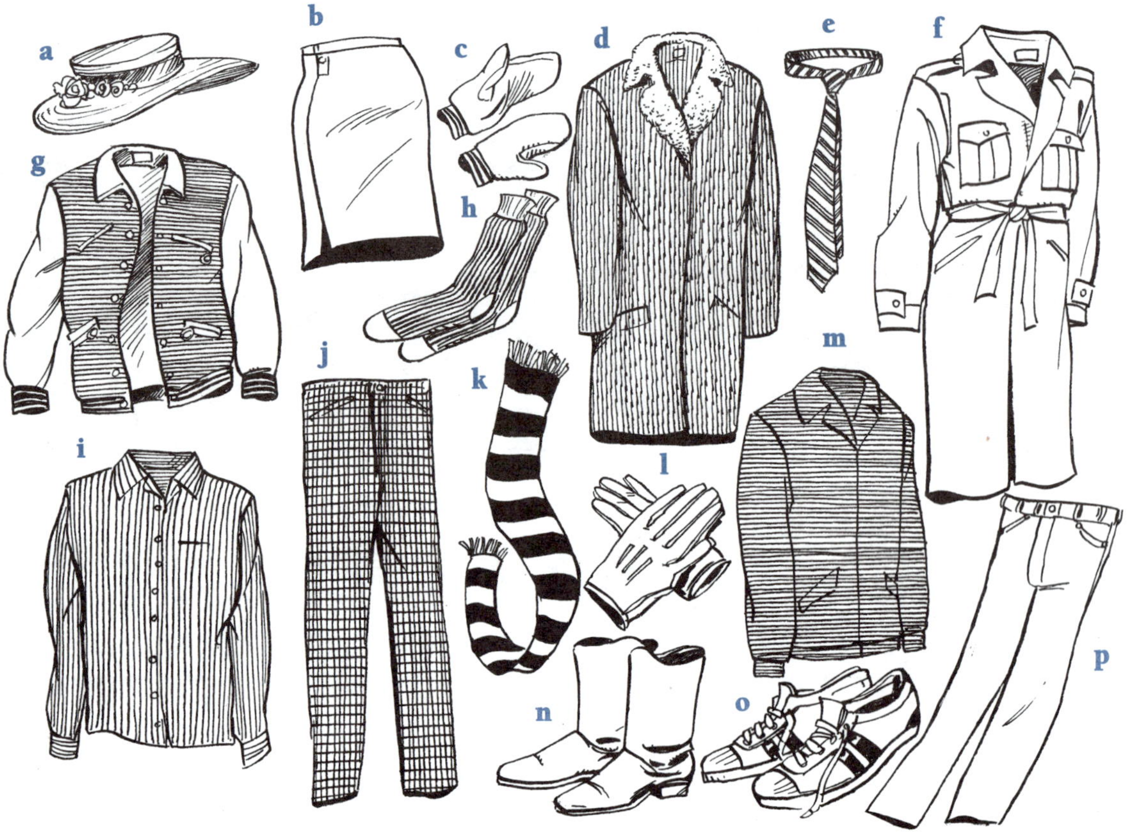

1. socks	5. jeans	9. a hat	13. a scarf
2. sneakers	6. mittens	10. a tie	14. a shirt
3. a jacket	7. boots	11. pants	15. gloves
4. a raincoat	8. a coat	12. a skirt	

West Edmonton Mall is the largest shopping centre in Canada. It has over 800 stores and many services. Every year half a million people shop there.

WHAT ARE THEY WEARING?

A Look at the picture. Describe what each person is wearing.

Olga Masha Max

Jun

Michel

Ana

Mona

Carlos Lili Kate

B Read about the people. Write their names.

1. I am a student. I am wearing jeans and a sweater. I am also wearing socks and sneakers. Who am I?

2. I work in a bank. I am wearing a blouse and a skirt. Who am I?

3. It is cool and rainy today. I am wearing a raincoat. I am also wearing rain boots. I am carrying an umbrella. Who am I?

4. I work in an office. I am wearing a jacket and pants. I am also wearing a white shirt and a tie. Who am I?

5. I work in a store. Today I am wearing pants and a sweater. I am also wearing a scarf. Who am I?

6. Today it is cold outside. I am wearing a winter coat and boots. I am wearing gloves on my hands. Who am I?

7. It is warm today. I am wearing shorts and a T-shirt. I am also wearing sock and sneakers and a sun hat. Who am I?

8. It is sunny today. I am wearing a T-shirt and pants and sunglasses. Who am I?

9. It's nice outside today, but it's a bit cool. I'm wearing a shirt and pants. I have a sweater, too.

10. It's nice out today. I'm wearing a T-shirt and a long skirt. Who am I?

TALK ABOUT IT

Work in a group. Talk about these questions.

1. How often do you shop for clothes?

2. Where do you shop?

3. What kind of clothes do you usually wear?

SURVEY: DIFFERENT KINDS OF CLOTHES

Copy the chart. Talk to six people. Write the information in the chart.

Ask: What do you wear at school?

Say: I wear…

Name						
at school						
to a party						
to work						
to a movie						
at home						
in winter						
in summer						

Present Continuous Aspect

Use the present continuous for actions that are in progress now.

> I'm looking for my shoes right now.

Use the present continuous for temporary situations.

> Some people are wearing short skirts this year.

To form the present continuous, put the auxiliary verb **be** before the main verb. Add **ing** to the verb. The ending **ing** shows continuous action. The auxiliary **am**, **is** or **are** shows present time.

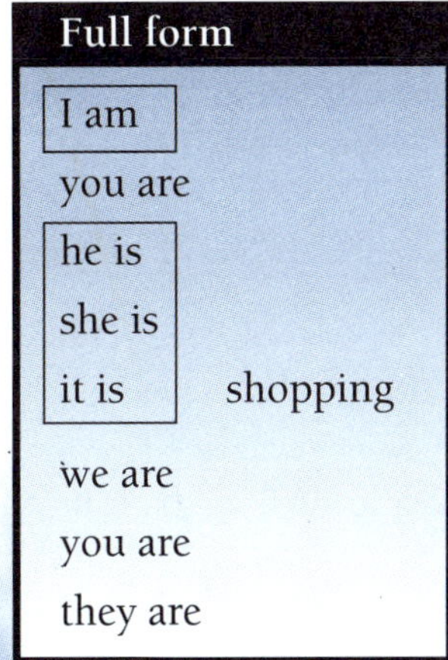

Full form	
I am	
you are	
he is	
she is	
it is	shopping
we are	
you are	
they are	

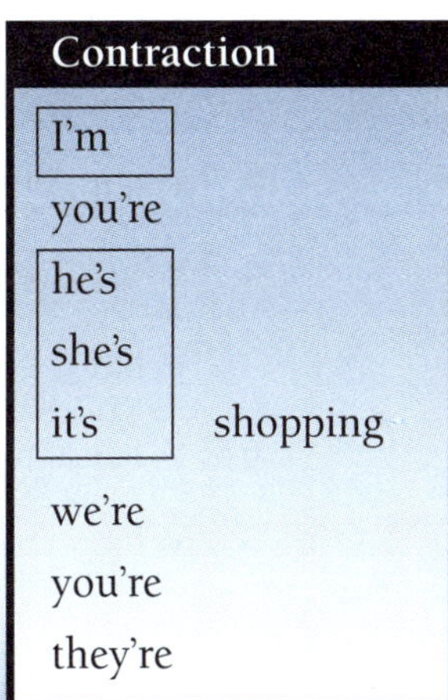

Contraction	
I'm	
you're	
he's	
she's	
it's	shopping
we're	
you're	
they're	

A Choose the verb and put it in the present continuous.

talk   wait   help   sell   pay   buy   try on

cash

credit card/debit card

Today the department store is having a sale. They **1**___________ coats and dresses for 50 percent off. Kate is shopping for a new coat. Lili **2**___________ her find a coat.

Ana and Mona are also at the department store. Ana **3**___________ a dress. Mona **4**___________ in line to pay for a new blouse. A woman near her **5**___________ to a friend. They **6**___________ some T-shirts. They **7**___________ for them with a credit card.

B Some sentences are wrong. Find the errors in the verbs and correct them.

> Carlos **is** buying some jeans.
> ᐱ

1.   Carlos and Ana shopping in a shoe store.

2.   Lili is buying a new dress.

3.   Masha are trying on boots.

4.   Max paying with his credit card.

5.   Michel is looking for a new jacket.

6.   I shopping in the same store.

7.   Jun is waiting to pay for his shirt.

8.   Kate and Mona is leaving the store.

9.   Olga carrying a shopping bag.

10.   A clerk is putting Jun's jacket into a bag.

C Look at the pictures on page 137. Match the questions to the answers.

1.   What is Lili doing?   a)   He's looking for a jacket.

2.   What is Kate doing?   b)   She's trying on shoes.

3.   What is Jun doing?   c)   She's waiting in line.

4.   What is Olga doing?   d)   He is looking at T-shirts.

5.   What is Max doing?   e)   He's trying on a coat.

6.   What is Michel doing?   f)   She's looking at dresses.

7.   What are Ana and Carlos doing?   g)   They are buying jeans.

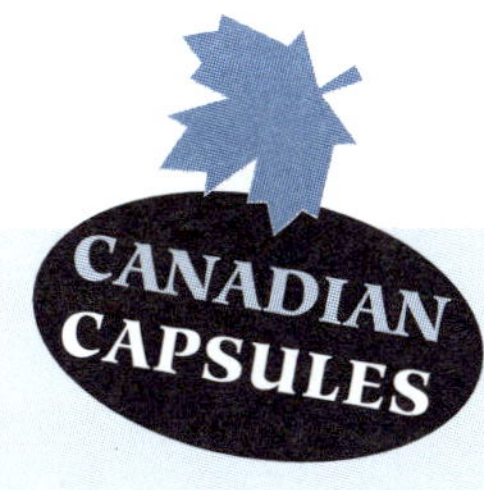

CANADIAN CAPSULES

One of Canada's largest department stores is The Bay. This store began in the early days in Canada, as the Hudson's Bay Company. It was so important that it printed its own money.

AT THE STORE

LISTENING ACTIVITY 17

A   Match the pictures to the words.

1. fitting room
2. small/medium/large
3. Try it on

4. It comes in black and white.
5. a mirror.

B   Read the questions with a partner.

C   Listen to the conversations. Answer the questions.

Mona

1. What does Mona like?
2. What colours does it come in?
3. What colour does Mona like?

Michel

1. What is Michel looking for?
2. What size is the first sweater?
3. What size does Michel wear?
4. What does Michel do?

Turn to page 144 for Exercise D.

WHAT SIZE DO YOU WEAR?

A Match the numbers to the pictures. Practise saying the numbers.

1. ¼ 2. ½ 3. ¾

a b c

B Match these symbols to the words.

1. S   a) large
2. M   b) extra small
3. L   c) extra large
4. XL   d) medium
5. XS   e) small

C Work in pairs to exchange information.

Partner A: You have information about Robert's sizes. Ask about Michel's sizes. Copy your chart and complete it.

Partner B: Turn to page 145.

Partner A

Ask: What size shoes does Michel wear? What size are Michel's shoes?

Say: Robert wears size 9 shoes.

Robert		Michel	
shoe	9	shoe	_____
glove	8	glove	_____
sweater	XL	sweater	_____
jacket	42	jacket	_____
hat	7 ¼	hat	_____
waist	40	waist	_____
ring	8 ½	ring	_____
shirt	17	shirt	_____

TALK ABOUT IT

1. Imagine you are shopping with a friend. You see something you want to buy. Talk about what you want. Talk about price, size, colour, etc.

2. Write a dialogue. One person is a shopper. The other person is a sales clerk. Act out your dialogue.

HOW TO WASH CLOTHES

A   Look at the pictures. Match the words to the pictures.

1. a washing machine
2. a dryer
3. white clothes
4. coloured clothes
5. laundry detergent
6. a dial
7. coins
8. a lever
9. a clothesline
10. clothespins
11. a laundry basket

B Read with your partner.

How to Use a Washing Machine

It is easy to wash your clothes. To begin, separate your clothes. Put the white clothes in one group. Put the clothes with colours such as red, green, or blue in another group.

Put the white clothes into the washing machine. Then put in the detergent. Next, choose the water temperature. To choose the water temperature, turn the dial. Use hot water for the white clothes. Then, put in the money. Last, push the lever to start the machine.

After the white clothes are finished, wash the coloured clothes the same way. Use cool or cold water for the coloured clothes.

When you have finished, put the clothes in the dryer to dry; or, if it is a sunny, warm day, you can hang the clothes on the clothesline outside.

C  Work with a partner. Put the steps in order.

1. Put in the money.
2. Put in the detergent.
3. Separate the clothes into groups.
4. Put the clothes in the dryer or on the clothesline.
5. Choose the water temperature.
6. Put the clothes in the washing machine.
7. Turn the dial to choose the water temperature.
8. Push the lever to start the machine.

D Close your book. Tell your partner how to wash clothes.

JOURNAL

A  Read the sentences. Close your book. Listen to the teacher. Write the sentences in your notebook.

> I'm Lili. I work in a bank. I wear a skirt and blouse or a suit to work. On the weekends, I wear jeans and a T-shirt.

B  What kind of clothes do you wear? Write about you, and what you wear.

TEN-MINUTE GAMES AND ACTIVITIES

Spot the Differences

Look at the two pictures. Find ten things that are different.

1.   Olga   Lili   Kate   Michel   Ana   Mona   Carlos   Jun

Masha   Max

2.   Olga   Lili   Kate   Michel   Ana   Mona   Carlos   Jun

Masha   Max

Quick Review

How many questions can you answer? Don't look back at the unit.

Work in teams. The first team to answer all the questions correctly wins.

1. Find three things we wear on our feet.

2. What is the name of a $1 coin?

3. What extra cost do you pay when you buy things in Canada?

4. What kind of machines can we use to wash and dry clothes?

5. What kind of soap do we use to wash clothes?

6. How much is a dime?

7. If you had three quarters, two dimes, and a nickel, how much money would you have?

8. Name three kinds of clothes people wear in winter to keep warm.

9. If you had a nickel and three pennies, how much money would you have?

10. Name the kind of coat you can wear in the rain.

11. What are two ways you can dry your clothes?

12. What are two things you can wear around your neck?

13. What kind of shoes can you wear to do sports?

14. Where can you try on clothes in a store?

15. What colour clothes do we wash with hot water?

Game: What Are You Wearing Today?

Students look around the room to see what people are wearing.

Student A goes to the front of the room, and stands with his or her back to the others. Students take turns asking questions to test Student A's memory.

Is Alex wearing a blue T-shirt?

Is Susan wearing a green sweater?

Student A answers "yes" or "no," until he or she makes a mistake. Then another student takes a turn.

The student with the most correct answers wins.

HOW MUCH IS IT?

LISTENING ACTIVITY 16

C   Listen and write the words. Use the worksheet.

Olga

Olga: I like __________ blue jacket. How much is __________, please?

Clerk: It's __________.

Olga: Oh, that's expensive.

Clerk: This one isn't as expensive.

Olga: How much is it?

Clerk: It's __________.

Olga: I like it. I think I'll take it.

Clerk: That comes to __________, with tax.

Max

Max: I __________ this black sweater. How much __________ it cost?

Clerk: It's __________.

Max: Oh, that's expensive.

Clerk: __________ one is only __________.

Max: Yeah, it's nice. I'll __________ it.

Clerk: That comes to __________ with tax.

D   Practise the conversation with a partner.

AT THE STORE

LISTENING ACTIVITY 17

D   Practise the conversations with a partner.

Mona

Clerk: Can I help you?

Mona: Yes, I like this blouse. It's beautiful.

Clerk: Yes, it is. It comes in red or blue.

Mona: I like the blue one. Can I try it on?

Clerk: Of course. The fitting room is right here.

Michel

Clerk: Can I help you?

Michel: Yes, I'm looking for a sweater.

Clerk: How about this one?

Michel: That's nice. What size is it?

Clerk: It's small.

Michel: Oh, I wear large. Do you have it in large?

Clerk: Yes, we do. This one is large.

Michel: I like this one. I'll try it on.

WHAT SIZE DO YOU WEAR?

Partner B

You have information about Michel's sizes. Give the information to your partner. Then get information about Robert's sizes.

Copy your chart and complete it.

Ask: What size shoes does Robert wear? What size are Robert's shoes?

Say: Michel wears size 11 shoes.

Robert		Michel	
shoe	_______	shoe	11
glove	_______	glove	$7\frac{1}{2}$
sweater	_______	sweater	M
jacket	_______	jacket	38
hat	_______	hat	$7\frac{3}{8}$
waist	_______	waist	38
ring	_______	ring	8
shirt	_______	shirt	$15\frac{1}{2}$

KINDS OF JOBS

 **A** Match the information about jobs. Write sentences.

> An orderly helps patients in a hospital.

a server	fixes cars	in a bank
a teller	types letters	in a hospital
a hairdresser	gives medicine	in a drugstore
a nurse	cuts hair	in a garage
a secretary	sells clothes	in a restaurant
a sales clerk	cashes cheques	in a salon
a pharmacist	serves food	in a store
a mechanic	helps patients	in an office

B   Look at the pictures. Write the names of the jobs.

a cook	an engineer	a nurse	a waiter/server
a doctor	a pharmacist	a taxi driver	a cashier
a mechanic	an accountant	a bank teller	a dentist
a hairdresser	a letter carrier	a secretary	a firefighter
a sales clerk	an orderly	a police officer	a day-care worker

GRAMMAR FOCUS   **Indefinite Articles**

	Before a consonant	Before a vowel
Singular Noun a/an	a cook	an electrician
Plural Noun Ø	cooks	electricians

Wrong ✘ I am cook.	Wrong ✘ I am electrician.
Right ✔ I am a cook.	Right ✔ I am an electrician.

A Answer the questions with one or more jobs. Use **a** or **an**.

> She works in a hospital. What is she?
> **a nurse, a doctor, an orderly**

1. He works in a restaurant. What is he?

2. She works in a day-care centre. What is she?

3. He works in a garage. What is he?

4. She works in a supermarket. What is she?

5. She works in a bank. What is she?

6. He works in a drugstore. What is he?

7. She works in a school. What is she?

8. He works in an office. What is he?

9. He works in a store. What is he?

10. He works in a salon. What is he?

WHAT DO YOU DO?

LISTENING ACTIVITY 18

A   Read the questions with a partner.

B   Listen and answer the questions.

Lili and Carlos

1. What is Lili's job?
2. Where does she work?
3. Where does Carlos work?
4. What is his job?
5. Where does Ana work?
6. What does she sell?
7. What is her job?

Jun, Michel, and Mona

1. What is Michel's job?
2. Where does he work?
3. What is Jun's job?
4. What does Mona do?
5. Where do Jun and Mona work?

Turn to page 162 for Exercise C.

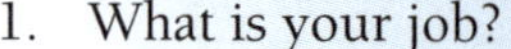

TALK ABOUT IT

Work in a group. Discuss these questions. If you don't have a job, talk about a job you would like to have.

1. What is your job?   (a taxi driver, a mechanic)
2. Where do you work?   (in a hospital, in a factory)
3. What do you do?   (serve people, answer the phone)

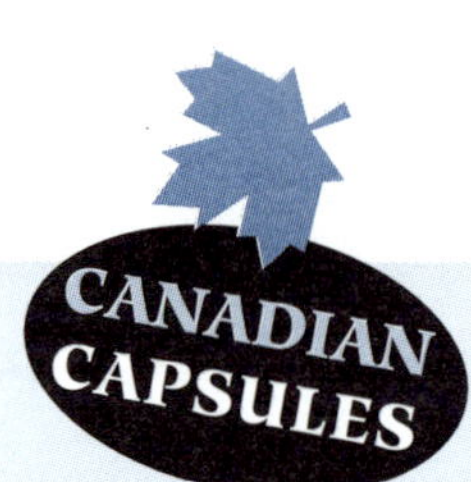

CANADIAN CAPSULES

If you are looking for a job in Canada, you can look in the classified section of newspapers. It is also a good idea to talk to people you know, to find out if they know about any jobs.

SURVEY: FAMILY JOBS

Walk around the classroom. Talk to six people. Find out about jobs that they have or that people in their families have. Write the jobs in the chart.

> **Ask:**   What do you do?
>
> What does your (mother, father, sister) do?
>
> **Answer:** I'm a…. I work in a….
>
> She's/He's a…. She/He works in a….

	Name	Jobs
1.		
2.		
3.		
4.		
5.		
6.		

"Can" to Express Ability

Use **can** before a main verb to show ability.

> He **can speak** English.
> I **can play** the guitar.

After **can**, use the base form of the verb (no ending).

> Wrong ✗ She can plays the guitar.
> Right ✔ She can play the guitar.

Affirmative
I can
you can
he can
she can
it can   swim
we can
you can
they can

A Write these sentences with the auxiliary verb **can**.

1. Lili plays the piano.
2. Carlos does taxes.
3. Kate drives a car.
4. Jun plays soccer.
5. Mona and Ana play tennis.
6. Masha plays the violin.
7. Max drives a taxi.
8. Michel cooks rice.
9. Henri puts out a fire.
10. Nick and George serve food.

"Can": Negative Form

Add **not** to **can** = **cannot**.

> I **cannot** speak Greek.
> I **can't** speak Greek.

Negative full form		Negative contraction	
I cannot		I can't	
you cannot		you can't	
he cannot		he can't	
she cannot		she can't	
it cannot	swim	it can't	swim
we cannot		we can't	
you cannot		you can't	
they cannot		they can't	

A Write negative sentences. Use contractions.

> We can see it. **We can't see it.**

1. Lili can speak Spanish.
2. Max can drive a bus.
3. Ana can type.
4. They can read French.
5. We can cook.
6. Carlos can play piano.
7. I can open the door.
8. Mona can swim.
9. Kate can use a fax machine.
10. Michel can use a computer.

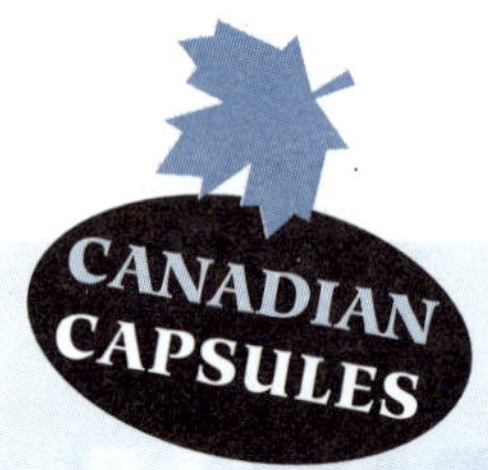

In Canada, it is illegal to ask personal questions about age, race, or religion at a job interview.

"Can": Question Form

Use **can** before the subject to form a question. Use the base form of the main verb after **can**.

> Can you speak English?

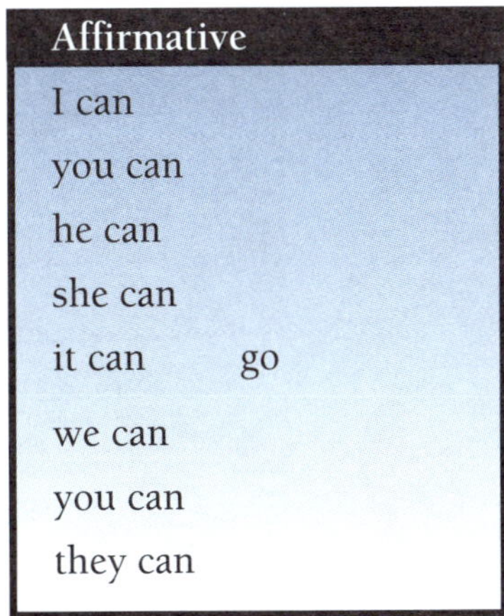

Affirmative
I can
you can
he can
she can
it can   go
we can
you can
they can

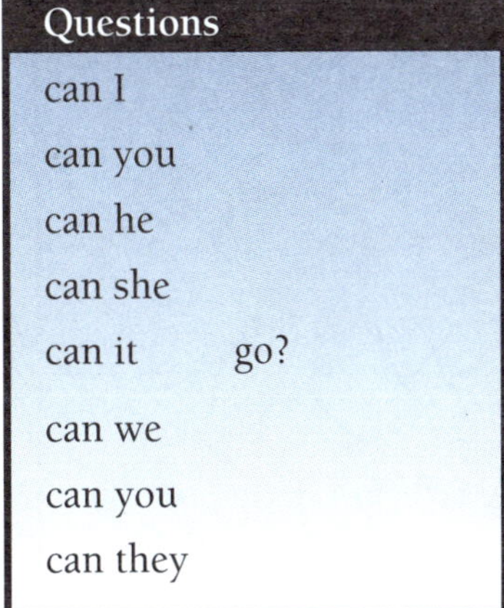

Questions
can I
can you
can he
can she
can it   go?
can we
can you
can they

TALK ABOUT IT

Talk to six people. Talk about some things you can do, and some things you can't do.

Ask: Can you…?

Say: I can…. I can't…..

SURVEY: WHAT CAN YOU DO?

A   Survey four students. Find out what they can and can't do. Add three items of your own.

Name				
1. play tennis				
2. speak two languages				
3. cook				
4. use a computer				
5. drive a car				
6. play soccer				
7. use a camera				
8. swim				
9. play piano				
10. drive a truck				
11. sing well				
12. use a washing machine				
13. speak Italian				
14.				
15.				
16.				

B   Report on the information. Write ten sentences about people in the class. Write the things they can and can't do.

> Marie can ride a bicycle.
>
> Peter can't play the violin.

WHAT'S MY JOB?

A   Read about the people. Find their jobs.

1. This person can help you when you want to look different. When your hair is too long, or you don't like the style, this person can cut it. He or she can wash your hair and can even change the colour of your hair.

2. This person helps you when you are sick in the hospital. This person can give medicine and help the doctor. This person can also help patients feel comfortable. He or she can wash patients and help them eat.

3. This person drives a car all day. You can call this person to take you somewhere when you are in a hurry and you don't have a car. You can call this person on the telephone, and he or she will come to your house to get you. This person can take you where you want to go. You pay this person when you arrive.

4. When you go to a store to buy clothes, this person can help you find the right size and colour. When you buy clothes, you pay this person. Then he or she puts your clothes in a bag for you.

5. This person can help you with your money. When you want to keep your money in a safe place, you can go to the bank and this person can put your money in the bank. He or she can also help you pay your bills and can tell you how much money you have in your bank account.

6. This person can help you when you are sick and you need medicine. He or she can tell you how much medicine to take and when to take it. This person works all day, or at night. This person can answer questions about your medicine.

7. This person can help you when you have a toothache. You can make an appointment, and he or she will check and clean your teeth. If you have a toothache, this person can fix your tooth.

8. This person walks a lot. When it is hot or cold outside, even when it rains or snows, this person brings mail to people at their homes. He or she delivers letters, magazines and packages. You can see this person outside every day of the week.

B   Copy the chart. Write the jobs from page 155. Then write three things each person does.

	Job	Things the person does
1.		
2.		
3.		
4.		
5.		
6.		
7.		
8.		

SALARIES

This is an information exchange. Work with a partner.

Partner A: Look at the information below. Ask for information about the people on the right side of the chart. Complete the charts for the people's salaries.

Partner B: Turn to page 163.

Partner A

Ask: How much does Paula make?

Say: Lili makes….

Lili	$538	Paula	________
George	$463	Sylvia	________
Tan	$180	Nadine	________
Ben	$290	Joe	________
Michael	$487	Shirley	________
Cindy	$186	Andrea	________
Denis	$338	Carl	________

GETTING A JOB

A   Read the job ads.

Day-care worker
Part-time
Experience needed
Call 684-1982
$375/week

The Men's Shop
1650 Danon Street
Sales clerk
Thursday–Saturday
Apply in person

Cashier
Mario's Market
Monday–Thursday
$235/week
Call 731-9865

Server Needed
The Chicken Place
10:00–4:00 daily
Apply in person

Cook needed
Jacob's Restaurant
Weekends 5–11
$7.00 an hour
346-2143

Orderly
Small hospital
Experienced only
3 days/week
325-7874

Driver
Dino's Pizza
Call 936-0912
$6.50/hour

B   Work with an partner. Read the sentences and answer "yes" or "no." Correct the sentences that are wrong.

1.   The server works in the evening.

2.   The cook works on the weekends.

3.   The orderly works four days a week.

4.   The driver makes $6.00 an hour.

5.   The day-care worker needs experience.

6.   The cashier makes less than the day-care worker.

7.   "The Chicken Place" needs a server.

8.   The sales clerk sells women's clothing.

9.   The cook makes more than the driver.

10.   The cashier must apply in person.

APPLYING FOR A JOB

LISTENING ACTIVITY  19

A   Look at the picture. Where is Olga?

 **B**   Read the questions with a partner.

 **C**   Listen to the conversation and answer the questions.

1.   What is the job?

2.   Where did Olga work for three years?

3.   What are the hours?

4.   How many days a week is the job?

5.   What is the pay?

6.   What does she have to do to apply for the job?

7.   What day does she have to come in?

8.   What is the address?

Turn to page 162 for Exercise D.

TALK ABOUT IT

Work with a partner. Choose a job from the newspaper ads on page 157. Write a dialogue for a job interview. Act it out.

APPLICATION FORMS

Work in pairs. Use the worksheet.

A   Fill in the **first** application form about you.

B   Fill in the **second** application form about your partner. Ask your partner for information.

Employment Application

Name: ________________________   ________________________
       Last   First

Address: __________   ______________________________
          Number   Street

________________   ______________   ______________
City   Province   Postal code

Telephone: ________________

Birth date: ________________________

Social Insurance Number: ________________________

Do you have experience? Yes ______   No ______

Previous jobs: ____

____

Job Application

Social Insurance Number: ☐☐☐☐☐☐☐☐☐

Name: ☐☐☐☐☐☐☐☐☐ ☐☐☐☐☐☐☐☐ ☐☐☐
       Last   First   Middle initial

Address: ☐☐☐☐ ☐☐☐☐☐☐☐☐☐☐☐☐☐☐☐☐☐☐
          Number   Street

☐☐☐☐☐☐☐☐ ☐☐☐☐☐☐☐ ☐☐☐☐☐☐☐
City   Province   Postal code

Date of birth: ☐☐ ☐☐ ☐☐☐☐
               M   D   Y

Telephone number: ☐☐☐ ☐☐☐☐☐☐☐
                  area code   number

Most recent work: ________________________

Name of company: ________________________

Job details: ________________________

JOURNAL

A   Read the sentences. Close your book. Listen to the teacher. Write the sentences in your notebook.

I'm Olga. I have a new job. It is in a day-care centre. I work every afternoon, from 12:00 to 5:00. I like to work with children.

B   Write about a job you have or a job you would like to have.

TEN-MINUTE GAMES AND ACTIVITIES

Jobs

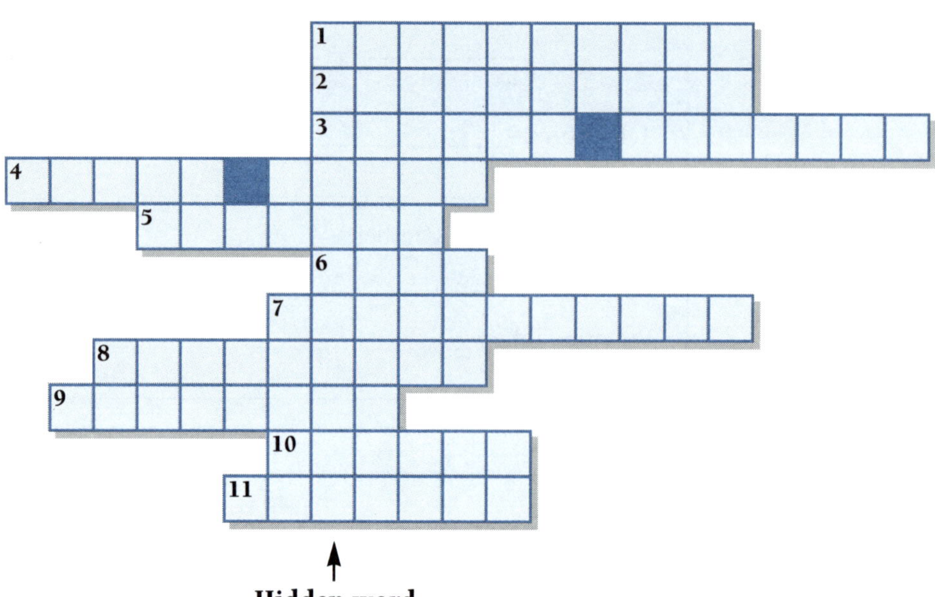

Complete the puzzle. Find the hidden word. Write it on the line. Use the worksheet.

1.   An _______________ works in an office. This person works with numbers, and helps people do their taxes.

2.   When you need medicine, you can ask this person for help.

3.   You call this person if you are in trouble or if someone does something wrong.

4.   This person helps you in a store.

5.   When you buy something in a store, this person takes your money and gives you change.

6.   This person prepares food for other people.

7.   His person helps you look better.

8. This person works in an office, typing letters and answering the telephone.

9. This person fixes your car.

10. This person helps you if you are sick.

11. This person helps you if you have a toothache.

Hidden word: When you apply for a job, you have to fill out an
________________ form.

Game: Jobs Tic-Tac-Toe

The class works in two teams. Team **X** and Team **O**.

A student from Team **X** begins by choosing a job from the grid below, and making a sentence about it. The student can talk about what a person does in the job or where the person works.

> A nurse works in a hospital.
>
> A nurse helps people.

If the student uses the word correctly, the teacher marks an **X** on the matching square on a grid on the board.

A student from Team **O** selects a square and makes a sentence in the same way. If the student uses the word correctly, the teacher marks an **O** in the matching square.

The first team to get three **X**s or three **O**s in a row wins. The rows can be vertical, horizontal or diagonal.

1.

accountant	mechanic	teacher
hairdresser	bank teller	cook
pharmacist	nurse	secretary

2.

server	cashier	police officer
dentist	taxi driver	firefighter
day-care worker	engineer	letter carrier

WHAT DO YOU DO?

LISTENING ACTIVITY 18

C Listen and write the words. Use the worksheet.

Lili and Carlos

Carlos: Hi, Lili. Do you ____________ a job?

Lili: Yes I ____________. I'm a bank teller. I ____________ in a bank downtown. What about you? ____________ you work?

Carlos: Yes, I do. I work in an office. ____________ an accountant.

Lili: I see. What about Ana? What ____________ she do?

Carlos: Ana ____________ in a store. She ____________ women's clothes. She's a sales clerk.

Jun, Michel, and Mona

Jun: Hi, Michel.

Michel: Hi, Jun. Hi, Mona.

Jun: Michel, do you ____________? Do you have a ____________?

Michel: Yes, I ____________ a job. I'm a cook in a restaurant. What about you, Jun?

Jun: ____________ an orderly in a hospital. Mona ____________ in a hospital too.

Michel: Really? What ____________ you ____________, Mona?

Mona: ____________ a nurse. I work in the hospital every evening.

D Practise the conversations with a partner.

APPLYING FOR A JOB

LISTENING ACTIVITY 19

D Practise the conversation with a partner.

Woman: Hello. Mrs. Peters speaking.

Olga: Hello. I'm calling about the ad for a job. It was in the newspaper yesterday.

Woman: Yes. It's for a day-care worker.

Olga: I'd like to apply.

Woman: Do you have experience working with children?

Olga: Yes, I do. I worked in a day-care centre for three years.

Woman: The job is part-time. The hours are 12:00 to 5:00.

Olga: Is that every day?

Woman: Yes, that's five days a week. The pay is $7.50 an hour.

Olga: That's fine.

Woman: If you want to apply, you have to fill out an application form. Can you come in on Tuesday?

Olga: Yes, of course.

Woman: The address is 637 Burrows Street. That's B-u-r-r-o-w-s.

SALARIES

Partner B

Give information about people on the left. Then ask for information about the people on the right. Complete the charts for the people's salaries.

Say: Paula makes….

Ask: How much does Lili make?

Paula	$438	Lili	_______
Sylvia	$871	George	_______
Nadine	$296	Tan	_______
Joe	$630	Ben	_______
Shirley	$581	Michael	_______
Andrea	$286	Cindy	_______
Carl	$199	Denis	_______

Community Contact Task 1

In the white pages of the telephone book, names are listed like this:

Family name	**Initial**
Nguyen	T

OR

Family name	**First name**
Weston	Elizabeth

Names are listed in alphabetical order. Barker comes before Martin because **B** is before **M** in the alphabet. Elizabeth Weston is listed before Francis Weston, because **E** is before **F** in the alphabet.

When three names begin with the same letter, they follow the order of the second letter in each name.

> Simpson
>
> Stevens
>
> Svenson

A Look in the telephone book. Find your family name. Answer these questions.

1. How many people have the same family name as you have?

2. Does anyone have your family name and your first name?

3. Does anyone have your family name and your initials?

B Look up three common family names. How many people can you count with these names?

Community Contact Task 2

Bring pictures of people in your family or of friends to class. Work in a group.

A Talk about a person in the picture.

1. What does the person look like?

2. What does the person do?

B Show your picture to the group. Ask people in the group to find the person.

Community Contact Task 3

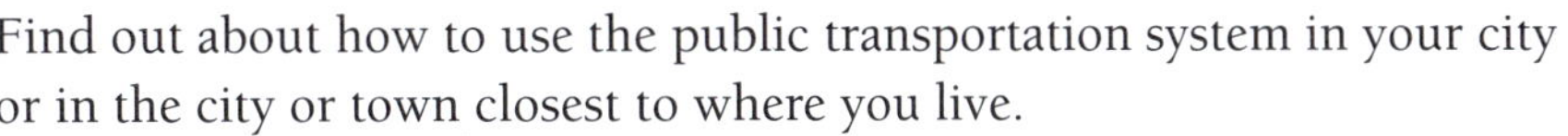

Find out about how to use the public transportation system in your city or in the city or town closest to where you live.

1. Who did you ask?

    a) the bus driver

    b) a Canadian friend

    c) a classmate

    d) other

2. How much do you pay for each of the following?

    a) cash fare

    b) tickets or tokens

    c) a pass

3. Can you transfer:

    a) between buses?

    b) from bus to subway?

    c) from subway to bus?

4. How long is a transfer valid?

5. What times does the transportation system start in the morning?

6. What times does the transportation system close at night?

7. How many seats does the bus have?

8. How do you open the door?

    a) push a gate

    b) push the door

    c) stand on the step

9. What colour are the buses?

10. What does the bus driver wear?

    a) a hat

    b) a tie

    c) a jacket

    d) a blue shirt

Community Contact Task 4

Go to a supermarket. Find the items on the list. Write the information in the chart. Use the worksheet.

Item	Name	Price
2 fruits		
2 green vegetables		
2 cold foods		
2 kinds of meat		
1 kind of fish		
2 foods that are red		
2 things to drink		
2 things that are not food		

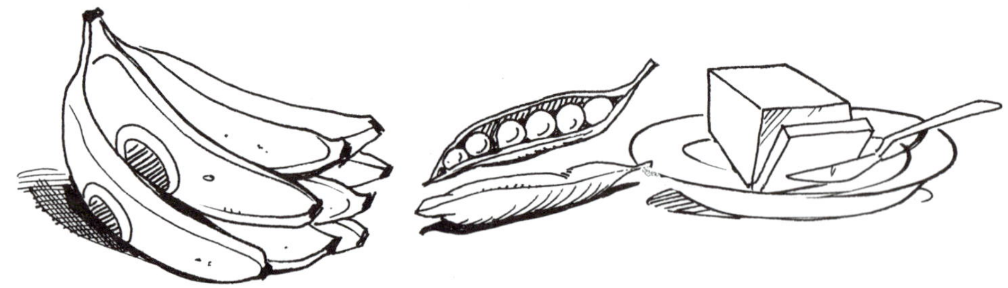

Community Contact Task 5

You are inviting three friends to your apartment for dinner. You want to cook a nice meal. You have $50 to spend. Go to the supermarket to check prices. Bring your menu to class, with lists of ingredients you will need. Write the price beside each ingredient you need to buy.

> 2 packages of noodles   **$2.79**

Community Contact Task 6

Imagine that you have a new apartment. You have $700 to buy furniture. Check prices in a furniture store or the furniture department of a department store. Compare these prices with second-hand furniture prices. To find second-hand furniture, you can look at the bulletin board at the supermarket or in the newspaper under Used Furniture or Garage Sales.

Complete a chart similar to the one below. Then decide which are the best pieces of furniture to buy for $700.

Furniture	New	Second-hand
Bed		
Table		
Chair		

Community Contact Task 7

Where do you think you could find an application form? Some possible places would be a bank, a fitness club, or a tourist bureau.

Find an application form. Fill it in. Then bring the application form to class. Compare the information asked for on your form with other application forms.

Appendix

Letters of the Alphabet

Print

Aa Bb Cc Dd Ee Ff Gg Hh Ii Jj Kk Ll Mm Nn Oo Pp Qq Rr Ss Tt Uu Vv Ww Xx Yy Zz

Write

Aa Bb Cc Dd Ee Ff Gg Hh Ii Jj Kk Ll Mm Nn Oo Pp Qq Rr Ss Tt Uu Vv Ww Xx Yy Zz

Cardinal Numbers

1	one	26	twenty-six	51	fifty-one	76	seventy-six
2	two	27	twenty-seven	52	fifty-two	77	seventy-seven
3	three	28	twenty-eight	53	fifty-three	78	seventy-eight
4	four	29	twenty-nine	54	fifty-four	79	seventy-nine
5	five	30	thirty	55	fifty-five	80	eighty
6	six	31	thirty-one	56	fifty-six	81	eighty-one
7	seven	32	thirty-two	57	fifty-seven	82	eighty-two
8	eight	33	thirty-three	58	fifty-eight	83	eighty-three
9	nine	34	thirty-four	59	fifty-nine	84	eighty-four
10	ten	35	thirty-five	60	sixty	85	eighty-five
11	eleven	36	thirty-six	61	sixty-one	86	eighty-six
12	twelve	37	thirty-seven	62	sixty-two	87	eighty-seven
13	thirteen	38	thirty-eight	63	sixty-three	88	eighty-eight
14	fourteen	39	thirty-nine	64	sixty-four	89	eighty-nine
15	fifteen	40	forty	65	sixty-five	90	ninety
16	sixteen	41	forty-one	66	sixty-six	91	ninety-one
17	seventeen	42	forty-two	67	sixty-seven	92	ninety-two
18	eighteen	43	forty-three	68	sixty-eight	93	ninety-three
19	nineteen	44	forty-four	69	sixty-nine	94	ninety-four
20	twenty	45	forty-five	70	seventy	95	ninety-five
21	twenty-one	46	forty-six	71	seventy-one	96	ninety-six
22	twenty-two	47	forty-seven	72	seventy-two	97	ninety-seven
23	twenty-three	48	forty-eight	73	seventy-three	98	ninety-eight
24	twenty-four	49	forty-nine	74	seventy-four	99	ninety-nine
25	twenty-five	50	fifty	75	seventy-five	100	one hundred

Ordinal Numbers

1st first	11th eleventh	21st twenty-first
2nd second	12th twelfth	22nd twenty-second
3rd third	13th thirteenth	23rd twenty-third
4th fourth	14th fourteenth	24th twenty-fourth
5th fifth	15th fifteenth	25th twenty-fifth
6th sixth	16th sixteenth	26th twenty-sixth
7th seventh	17th seventeenth	27th twenty-seventh
8th eighth	18th eighteenth	28th twenty-eighth
9th ninth	19th nineteenth	29th twenty-ninth
10th tenth	20th twentieth	30th thirtieth
		31st thirty-first

Days of the Week

Monday	(Mon.)
Tuesday	(Tues.)
Wednesday	(Wed.)
Thursday	(Thurs.)
Friday	(Fri.)
Saturday	(Sat.)
Sunday	(Sun.)

Months of the Year

January	(Jan.)
February	(Feb.)
March	(Mar.)
April	(Apr.)
May	
June	
July	
August	(Aug.)
September	(Sept.)
October	(Oct.)
November	(Nov.)
December	(Dec.)

Shapes

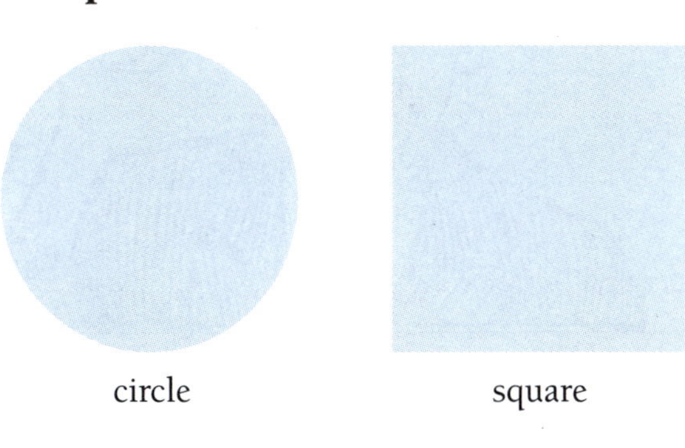

circle   square

rectangle

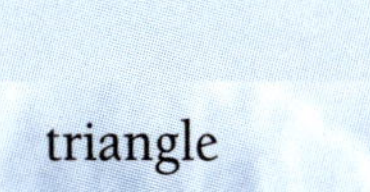

triangle

GOODBYE.
'BYE.
GOOD-
BYE.
GOOD-
BYE.
GOODBYE.
'BYE.
GOOD-
BYE.
'BYE.
'BYE.

Englisch ist einfach

ben englizce oranmak stiurum

私は英語が好きです。

أنا أحب هذا الكتاب

Vaya suka buku ini

Bu Kitapi cok seudim

See you in Canadian Concepts 3 !

Delam mikhad englisi yad begiram

Mi piace molto questo
libro

我會說英文

Tôi thích quyển sách này

Inglês é fácil de aprender.

Je parle l'anglais

안녕

私はこの本が大好きです。

Μιλαω Εγγλινικά

ME GUSTA HABLAR INGLES

Μου αρέσει αυτό το βιβλίο